Women on the Hill

A History of Women in Congress

Jill S. Pollack

Women Then—Women Now

Franklin Watts
A Division of Grolier Publishing
New York / London / Hong Kong / Sydney
Danbury, Connecticut

To Alexandra, Trevor, Kyle, and Grant

You must do the thing you think you cannot do.
—Eleanor Roosevelt

Interior Design by Molly Heron
Photo credits ©: AP/Wide World Photos: 79, 165; Archive Photos: 52, 68; Reuters/Bettmann: 136, 158, 162, 173, 180; UPI/Bettmann: 23, 27, 28, 35, 41, 48, 57, 60, 63, 66, 74, 80, 85, 94, 100, 107, 113, 116, 126, 131, 135, 139, 146, 154, 176.

Library of Congress Cataloging-in-Publication Data
Jill S. Pollack.
Women on the Hill: A History of Women in Congress / by Jill S. Pollack
p. cm. — (Women then—women now)
Includes bibliographical references and index.
Summary: Describes the historic, ongoing struggle of women to find equal representation in national politics, including short biographies of prominent congresswomen, an analysis of special roles of women in Congress, and a summary of how that legislative body works.
ISBN 0531-11306-X
1. Women legislators—United States—History—Juvenile literature. 2. Women legislators—United States—Biography—Juvenile literature. 3. Women in politics—United States—History—Juvenile literature. 4. United States. Congress—Biography—Juvenile literature. 5. United States. Congress—History—Juvenile literature. [1. Women legislators—History. 2. Legislators. 3. United States. Congress—Biography. 4. Women—Biography. 5. Women in politics. 6. United States. Congress—History.] I. Title. II. Series.
E747.P65 1996
328.73'0082—dc20 96-33831 CIP AC

Printed in the United States of America.

1 2 3 4 5 6 7 8 9 10 R 05 04 03 02 01 00 99 98 97 96

Contents

Acknowledgments

I WOULD LIKE to extend my gratitude to the following people and organizations for their assistance on the research and writing of this book:

Russell Primm and David Strass of Franklin Watts for their diligent guidance and editorial talents; Louise Quayle, agent extraordinaire; the Iowa Legislature Information Office for permission to adapt their graphical representation of how a bill becomes a law; Hope Chamberlain, whose book *A Minority of Members* provided a wealth of information and insight into women in politics through 1972; and, of course, my partner Jackie for all her love and support.

A special debt is owed to the strong, wise, and willful women in Congress—past, present, and future.

Foreword

WHY READ A book about women in Congress?

First, these are interesting people. They are pioneers who entered America's highest lawmaking institution when very few women held elective office at any level. They are self-confident, gutsy women who overcame the historical prejudices and barriers that had kept most women out of politics. They dared to clear pathways into what had been (and largely remains) men's territory.

The stories of women in Congress tell us it is possible to do what had been thought almost impossible. Because female candidates have won campaigns and served successfully in elective office, today's young women more easily imagine themselves as public leaders. Young men, too, need not carry the baggage of ignorance and prejudice about women's abilities that narrowed the vision of previous generations.

In addition to opening the political world to other women, congresswomen have brought new outlooks and issues to the table. For a variety of complex reasons (about which volumes have been written), life is quite different for the two sexes. Research conducted by the Center for the American Woman and Politics at Rutgers University's Eagleton Institute of Politics reveals a difference in attitudes on public policy issues between female and male elected officials even in the same political party. Women legislators place a higher priority on women's rights and issues related to women's traditional roles as caregivers and nurturers in their families and communities. These differences suggest that voters should compel voters to continue to elect both men and women to office in order that the government reflects the diverse concerns of its citizens.

In 1996, women hold only a little more than 10 percent of the 535 seats in the U.S. House and Senate—but they are a rich mixture. They come from different social classes, family experiences, races, ethnicities, religious affiliations, and political parties. They are Democrats and Republicans. They range in age from 35 to 75. They have worked as lawyers, teachers, social workers, businesswomen, and health professionals. Some are married, others are widowed, divorced, or single. A few are new mothers; others have older children or no children. The arrival of women in politics has shown not only that men and women can both hold office, but that a rich mixture of people can work together for the greater public good.

Americans want the noble concepts on which their country was founded—freedom, fairness, and opportunity—to translate into daily realities. It is not enough to talk about inclusion. In a huge and incredibly diverse nation, inclusion must be a way of life.

This book shows us progress. The very presence of women in high elected office demonstrates that as a society we can change, improve, become more inclusive. Slowly but surely, we can make room for all who have something to contribute and wish to participate.

—Ruth B. Mandel
Eagleton Institute of Politics, Rutgers University
New Brunswick, New Jersey

Introduction

THE WOMEN WHO have served in Congress have at least one thing in common—they are women. Beyond that, they are as diverse as the populations they serve. They are Democrats and Republicans, independent-minded and party loyal, urban and rural, liberal and conservative, quiet and outspoken. It's a miscalculation to assume that because they are women, these politicians will vote the same way on issues of war, abortion, civil rights, lesbian and gay rights, economic tariffs, foreign policy, judicial appointments, or even the Equal Rights Amendment.

In the first half of this century, many of these women found themselves with the title of representative or senator because they were filling the places of their deceased husbands. Politics was not their passion. But since the late 1960s a new breed of female politician has emerged. Past Speaker of the House Thomas P. ("Tip") O'Neill once noted, "All politics is local." His career in Congress spanned thirty-four years and his grasp of politics was right on target. Politics is based on local concerns: are the schools safe, are property taxes too high, are new developments helping to boost local economy, are new developments going to harm local economy? Even issues like garbage pickup can mushroom into community-wide discussions that lead to political change.

Women's involvement in local politics began long before the 1960s—before they even had the right to vote. Many urban women in the late 1800s got involved because of "local" concerns such as safety and health care for the poor. Most men were active in party-oriented politics rather than working on a particular issue. Over time, as Tip O'Neill's declaration suggests, the issues that local activists grappled with grew into the basis for politics on the national level.

Senator Barbara Mikulski got involved in politics because a highway was to be built through her ethnic Baltimore neighborhood. Senator Patty Murray got involved because a special school-related program was going to be cut. These senators, and many women like them, stepped forward to improve situations that affected their daily lives and those of their neighbors. The discovery that this type of activism yields results is enough to get many women interested in running for office. In social movement after social movement, women knocked on doors, wrote pamphlets, and performed all the tedious and necessary tasks needed to get the job done. Eventually, this experience helped many women gain the skills—and the confidence—necessary to be productive elected officials.

For some women activists of past generations, family wealth played a large role in determining a career in politics. Family connections, and especially family fortunes, can open doors that other people don't even know exist. Money contributed to a party or a candidate can have a strong ripple effect. Large donations are rarely forgotten and often repaid, one way or another. Also, without the need to worry about paying the bills, women from wealthy families were able to focus their attention on running for office.

Traditionally, family wealth was controlled by the male members of a family. Inheritances and economic control were passed from father to firstborn son. Daughters often received allowances but were able to exert little influence in financial matters. This meant that women who wanted to use their wealth to further their political careers had to seek "permission" from the men in their families to pursue their goals. At the very least, they needed tacit approval for their actions. Occasionally, there were exceptions to this rule. Frances Bolton, a Republican from Ohio, was left a large inheritance that she controlled. Millicent Fenwick, a Republican from New Jersey, was a millionaire in her own right.

Other women come to politics because they themselves have had financial difficulties and want to help others. California Representative Lynn Woolsey (D–Calif.; rep. 1993–) is the first to tell you that she was a welfare mother relying on government financial assistance. Today, she is on Capitol Hill working to help others in similar situations.

The women who choose to make politics their life's work are part of a long line of women activists from all socio-economic classes. In fact, without the hard work and sacrifice of our foremothers, women today wouldn't even be allowed to vote, let alone run for office!

Suffrage

Although women have always been involved in politics and society, they have not always enjoyed the same rights as men. Until this century, women had virtually no legal rights. They could not vote, hold elected office, own property, or inherit money. They had no rights over their children—if a husband chose, he could take the children away from home and forbid their mother to see them. When a woman married, it was thought that she and her husband would become "one." But that "one" was really the husband. If, for example, a woman inherited money from a deceased relative (assuming there were no male children to inherit) that money became the legal property of her husband.

It was not until the antislavery movement gained strength in the early 1800s that American women began to organize to improve their own lives. Deeply disturbed by the horrors of slavery, white women began to speak out and write on the subject. Two sisters, Sarah and Angelina Grimké, became well known for their antislavery views. They traveled to many states and spoke to the public and to state legislatures. Their efforts and activities interested many other women, and the scope of issues discussed expanded. In the 1840s a movement of activist women began to develop. Mostly middle class, these women took on issues ranging from slavery to temperance (restrictions on drinking alcohol) to the health and well-being of the growing numbers of women and children living in poverty.

When Lucretia Mott and Elizabeth Cady Stanton, two outspoken antislavery activists, traveled to London, England, to attend the World Antislavery Convention, the idea for women's rights moved to the top of their agenda. They arrived at the convention to find that the doors were closed to them—the event was for men only. The two activists, infuriated, returned to the United States with a strong purpose. They eventually organized the 1848 Seneca Falls Convention on Women's Rights. Out of this meeting in upstate New York grew the women's suffrage movement. (Suffrage means "the right to vote"; it comes from the Latin word *suffragium*, meaning "to express support.")

Other famous activists joined in the fight for women's rights. Susan B. Anthony and Victoria Woodhull contributed their talents in oratory and writing, helping more women to become aware of—and incensed at—the injustices in their own life situations.

Opinions varied on how to tackle the wide array of wrongs against women. Some believed in trying to revise the property and divorce laws. Others wanted to focus first on winning women the right to vote. Some leaders, like Stanton, believed in fighting for all people's rights at the same time.

This combination of anger and talent eventually led to the formation of two organizations dedicated to one purpose—a woman's right to vote. The National Woman Suffrage Association (NWSA) and the American Woman Suffrage Association (AWSA) were both formed in 1869, but they tackled the problem in different ways. The NWSA, led by Stanton, was more radical in its thought, while the AWSA favored a more conservative approach. Stanton was known for her fiery rhetoric and dramatic speeches. Behind her words was the clear message that women and African-Americans were equal to white men. For Stanton, the fight for women's suffrage was directly linked to the fight to end slavery. Leaders of the AWSA felt it was important to focus on one issue only, so they restricted their arguments to gaining the vote for women.

Since not all women think alike, these two groups were often at odds with each other as they set about building a national network of women activists. Eventually, they were able to overcome their differences. In 1890 the two groups merged into the National American Woman Suffrage Association. Their members traveled tirelessly from one end of the country to the other, organizing small local groups and speaking to public gatherings large and small. The first woman elected to Congress, Jeannette Rankin, spent years traveling through the state of Montana on behalf of women's suffrage.

This grassroots organizing was vitally important to the national effort. Grassroots means that local people lead the effort in their communities. Hundreds of small groups in different cities all fought for the same thing, but each group tailored the fight to its own community. Urban areas might connect women's suffrage to help for those living in poverty. Rural farming areas could address the rights women needed to run farms or businesses left to them.

Another important function of grassroots organizing is lobbying—trying to sway a member of government to one side of an issue. Since all politics is local, it's important that local residents lobby their representatives. For instance, a senator from Indiana would listen more closely to a constituent from Indianapolis than to someone from Minnesota. In the fight for suffrage, the individual state legislatures encountered heavy lobbying efforts.

But progress seemed too slow for Elizabeth Cady Stanton. She decided to run for Congress in 1866 as an Independent. Victoria Woodhull followed her lead and ran for the United States presidency in 1872. Needless to say, both women lost their bids for office. The public relations value, though, was immense. Their campaigns helped to raise awareness about the issue of women's suffrage.

In 1900 a new leader, Carrie Chapman Catt, came on the scene. She became the president of the National American Woman Suffrage Association and was able to meld the differing factions. Her leadership helped galvanize a nation of women (and many men). During the early 1900s, grassroots work from many communities combined into a national effort. Major protests and marches were held in Washington, D.C., and New York City; letters to the editor were published in hundreds of newspapers; town hall meetings were convened to discuss the matter; and members of Congress were lobbied by their constituents.

Finally in 1918 the U.S. House of Representatives passed the Nineteenth Amendment, stating, "The right of citizens of the United States to vote shall not be denied or abridged by the United States or by any state on account of sex." The Senate passed the same amendment in 1919. Then it was up to the states to ratify it. A constitutional amendment must be ratified, or approved, by a majority of the states to become effective.

The Numbers

The Tennessee legislature voted its approval of the Nineteenth Amendment in June 1920, seventy-two years after the Seneca Falls Convention. This state legislature was the last one necessary to make a majority of states in favor of the amendment. Legend has it that the state senator who cast the deciding vote did so because his mother called and told him to. Whatever his reasons, the long fight for suffrage had ended in triumph for the women of America.

But how much really changed? With the vote came a new sense of self for many women. New opportunities presented themselves as women began to get involved in activities outside the home. For those with an activist's heart, politics was very inviting. For those more comfortable with the way things had always been, change came more slowly.

Surprisingly, many women of the day didn't take advantage of their newfound right to vote. Only 25 percent of eligible women cast votes in the election of 1920. By 1952 that number had grown to 55 percent. Today, women make up 53 percent of the electorate and are courted by candidates because of their voting power.

Education and public discussion have increased the number of women voters. National groups such as the National Organization for Women and the League of Women Voters have helped women understand that they have a very important role in politics. State and local affiliates of these organizations, and others like them, rate candidates, donate money to campaigns, publish educational materials for voters, or provide networks to help women in politics to connect with one another.

In the first fifty-six years of women in Congress—1917 to 1973—only eleven women served in the Senate and eighty-one in the House of Representatives. It wasn't until 1983 that women comprised even 5 percent of a sitting Congress. In 1995, eight out of a hundred senators, or 8 percent, were women. In the House of Representatives, forty-eight of the 435 voting representatives were women, or just 11 percent. These numbers don't scream equality, and some might argue that women in elected political positions are lagging far behind women in business and the professions.

This news isn't new. Since the first Congress was convened in 1789, more than ten thousand men have served, compared with fewer than two hundred women. Congresswoman Martha Griffiths once asked the Library of Congress to calculate how long it would take at the current rate for women to gain parity with men in Congress. The answer was 432 years!

These numbers notwithstanding, the women who have gone to Washington to represent their districts or states have served with distinction. Their numbers may not be grand, but women in Congress have proven their knowledge of traditional issues such as economics and foreign affairs. They have also brought to light more social issues needing attention. In the 1920s the Sheppard-Towner Maternity and Infancy Aid Act, allocating congressional funds to help poor mothers and children, was pushed through by women. Massachusetts Representative Edith Nourse Rogers championed the plight of America's veterans and wrote the bill creating the national network of veterans' hospitals. In the 1970s, New York Representatives Geraldine Ferraro and Bella Abzug investigated the status of America's elderly. Hawaii Representative Patsy Mink worked to improve immigrants' rights. In the 1990s, Colorado Representative Pat Schroeder and several other women in both parties fought for families by co-sponsoring the Family and Medical Leave Bill mandating that companies allow employees time away from work to care for newborns or ill family members.

The women on the "Hill" (Capitol Hill) have also spent their years fighting against the subtle and overt sexism that permeates our society. When Representative Rankin made her Capitol Hill debut the newspapers labeled her an "Amazon"—what other kind of woman would want to dirty her hands in politics! Ohio Representative Frances Bolton, who served an esteemed fourteen terms in Congress, refused to be called a "congresswoman" because she couldn't find the word in the dictionary. And in 1992 a congressional clerk issuing ID cards assumed Illinois Senator Carol Moseley Braun was a congressman's spouse rather than a senator in her own right.

Patsy Mink, Pat Schroeder, New York Representative Shirley Chisholm, and many others were vocal supporters of a measure called Title IX that mandated equal educational opportunities for young women and men. And most (not all) of the women in Congress from Rankin to the present have supported the Equal Rights Amendment (ERA), which would grant equal rights to women and men in many areas of public and private life. This proposed amendment to the United States Constitution states: "Equality of Rights under the law shall not be denied or abridged by the United States or any state on account of sex." The ERA was passed by both houses of Congress in the early 1970s, but not enough states ratified it, so it has never been added to the Constitution, which uses only the pronoun "he."

Perhaps this will change in the years to come. Across the country, women are being elected in record numbers to city, county, and state positions of leadership. Many of these politicians will make bids to go to Washington to fight for reforms and to represent their districts. When their numbers equal those of their male colleagues, the women on the Hill will be a formidable force indeed!

1

Jeannette Rankin: The First Woman in Congress

When Jeannette Rankin (R–Mont.; rep. 1917–19, 1942–43)* walked into Congress on April 2, 1917, she was met with a standing ovation from the room full of men. But in the days and months preceding this event, she endured disdainful editorials from newspapers across the country; fictional accounts of her looks and her dressing habits; and articles calling her an "Amazon" and a "cowgirl." The expectation from some was that she was in Congress to find a husband. One reviewer even wrote that her "well-fitting garments" added to her feminine effect and that the V-neck opening of her dress served to distinguish her from her male colleagues covered at the neck by starched linen.[1]

Rankin was supported by the women in the suffrage movement and by many of the farmers and workers throughout the state of Montana who voted her into office. But she was also the target of naysay-

*Information in parentheses identifies political party, home state, and years of service as a representative and/or senator.

ers who prophesied that sending a woman into the male den that was Congress amounted to no less than the "feminization" of men and America. These detractors thought that a woman would surely wreak havoc in the comfortable, male halls of government.

On this last point, they were correct.

Born in 1880 to a hardworking couple who had moved to Montana as the American West was being settled, Jeannette Rankin was one of seven children in a very close-knit family. Everyone in the family attended university and became active in politics. John Rankin, Jeannette's father, was the county commissioner for six years before he died, her brother held elective office, and all of her siblings worked on her campaigns.

Unlike most other states, Montana had granted women the right to vote in elections. As Rankin described it, men and women in the West worked side by side because the work was so difficult. No one even had a chance to give much thought to gender equality. When she decided to run for the U.S. House of Representatives in 1916, Rankin already had an impressive political career. She was a tireless supporter of suffrage and traversed the state to build coalitions and grassroots organizations for the cause. She traveled to Boston and San Francisco, where she saw firsthand what life was like in poverty-stricken slums. She also spent time in Washington, D.C., lobbying on behalf of women and for suffrage.

Rankin carried these experiences and life lessons with her when she talked with voters throughout Montana. At the time, Montana was not divided into congressional districts. The state simply elected two representatives at large. Because the populations of states were smaller than they are today, a representative at large could generally do the work required in representing the whole state. But as an area's population grew, eventually states adopted districts and elected representatives to be voices just for the constituents who lived in that district.

In 1916, however, Rankin had to travel to little towns and hamlets, over plains and farmland, to talk to people. Her family helped in any way they could. Her brother Wellington was her campaign manager and longtime advisor, her sisters left their children at home and went out on the campaign trail for her, and even her aging mother traveled a bit to garner votes for her daughter.

When asked why a woman should be in government, Rankin's reply was, "There are hundreds of men to care for the nation's tariff and foreign policy and irrigation projects. But there isn't a single woman to look after the nation's greatest asset: its children."[2] In Congress, she would live up to her word by authoring the Sheppard-Towner bill. In her later years, Rankin voiced many more reasons women were needed in Congress. At one point, after living through two world wars, Rankin said, "Men have taught women not to trust their emotions. But women have an emotional ideal to contribute, and if they organized we could have peace in one year."[3]

During the campaign of 1917, the United States was poised to enter World War I in Europe. Rankin talked of the impending war and whether or not people wanted to see their sons and husbands go off to fight on foreign soil. Many of Montana's voters were understandably worried about the consequences of—and the reasons for—fighting such a war. Rankin shared their concern.

What set her apart was that she spoke to the women and the men of her state on equal terms. She fully understood that women were just as capable as men of making their own decisions and of understanding the issues of the day. In addition to the threat of war, taxes and working conditions were of great interest to people in the rural communities of Montana. Rankin told voters she was willing to fight to improve the tax structure, to limit the workday to eight hours for women, and, of course, to pass women's suffrage.

Her campaign persistence and her messages paid off. Montana sent the first woman to Congress, and Jeannette Rankin made sure she would not soon be forgotten. She had bested seven male candidates in the Republican primary and easily defeated the Democratic challenger, attorney George Farr. She received 76,932 votes to 66,974 for Farr.

The Continued Fight for Suffrage

After the initial interest of the press and the false newspaper accounts, Congress went to work. Rankin immediately kept her promises and began fighting for an eight-hour workday for women, better health care for women and children, a stronger national defense, and a national amendment for women's suffrage.

Rankin cosponsored a resolution drafting the Nineteenth Amendment to the Constitution—the amendment that granted women the right to vote. She was also savvy enough to stop a ploy by the Judiciary Committee when its members tried to have the resolution "killed." In Congress bills can be stalled for years, and eventually killed, if they never "make it out of committee." Each bill must be sent to a committee for research and discussion, but if the committee never votes on it, the bill will never go to the full House or Senate floor for a vote. Many controversial or partisan bills have died in this manner. (See "How

Jeannette Rankin, the first woman in Congress, in 1917

Does Congress Work?" to learn how a bill becomes a law.) Rankin's attentiveness kept the struggle for suffrage alive.

It's interesting to note that one of the major groups opposing suffrage was the leadership of the Southern states. The issue for them was not one of women, but rather of race. If women could vote, then more African-American women would vote. At that time in history, southern politicians considered African-Americans an "ignorant electorate" and did all they could to make it difficult for black men and women to vote.

In 1917 Representative Rankin had little patience for another argument being used against suffrage at that time. This argument held that a constitutional amendment giving women the vote was an infringement on the rights of individual states to govern as they see fit. When it was said that the state constitutions were developed by the people of that state and should be respected, Rankin countered, "May I ask who 'the people' are?" Of course, women had not been included in this equation.

The Price of an Independent Vote

In the spring of that year, just as Representative Rankin was beginning to make some headway with her legislative agenda, President Woodrow Wilson asked Congress to declare war on Germany. World War I was already raging in Europe, and Wilson was ready to assist America's allies. The problem for Rankin was that she was an avowed pacifist—she did not believe in war. She did, however, believe strongly that America should be well prepared to defend its shores if an invader threatened the country. But to be the aggressor, or to fight a war on foreign soil? To this she said no.

A role-call vote was taken in Congress on whether to declare war. When Rankin's name was called, she answered, "I wish to stand by my country, but I cannot vote for war. I vote 'No.'" She was not alone in this decision. A total of forty-nine other representatives (all men, of course) also voted against the war declaration, but Representative Rankin was singled out in the press and vilified before the whole country. She was labeled a traitor to America and used as an example of why women couldn't be effective in government.

In truth, it took great courage for her to vote her conscience when all those around her were urging each other to vote for war. Even her brother Wellington implored her to "vote like the men." But Representative Rankin felt she was sent to Congress to do what was right. And that's what she did.

The furor over this vote overshadowed the rest of her legislative record. In addition, the Montana legislature moved to create congressional districts. This meant that Rankin, a Republican, would have to run for reelection in a mainly Democratic area. Instead, she decided to run for the Senate.

A Bold Move

If the country had qualms about sending a woman to the House of Representatives, then it would certainly be disturbed by a woman in the Senate. The Senate was a bastion of masculinity, still called an "exclusive gentleman's club," that even Jeannette Rankin could not penetrate. She had no illusions about winning this election but felt that she would further the cause for women by at least running. When the votes were tallied she had not won, but she received many more votes than expected.

With such a defeat, many women would have bowed out of the political scene. But Rankin's convictions were strong, and she spent the next several decades working for various organizations that lobbied for suffrage, women's issues, and peace. During the Great Depression of the 1930s she often worked without pay, living on money she inherited from her father. With her public speeches she began to garner attention, and she started speaking out more strongly.

In the late 1930s war was raging again in Europe, but the American people did not want to become involved. Isolationists—those who believed that the United States should not get involved with the affairs of other countries—were strong voices on the streets and in government. Rankin was among them, as she did not believe in war except strictly in self-defense.

In 1940 many people agreed with Rankin's peace objectives. They rewarded her outspokenness by returning her to Congress—again on the eve of war. Sooner than anyone wished, another historic vote would be taken and, again, Rankin would provide a dissenting vote. This time it was December 7, 1941, and the Japanese had just bombed Pearl Harbor, an American naval base in Hawaii. There were no live television reports to confirm what had happened, only descriptions on the radio. The next day, President Franklin Delano Roosevelt immediately moved to declare war on Japan and thus become embroiled in World War II. With less than twenty-four hours to consider the issue, Congress voted on a declaration of war. The Senate voted unanimously to support it. The House of Representatives also voted. Rankin was the only member of Congress to vote against the declaration of war.

This time the press was a little more kind and admitted the courage of Representative Rankin. For her part, she reminded people that there was really very little information to go on, since only radio reports had come through from Pearl Harbor. But the country was unified behind the war effort the instant they learned of the Pearl Harbor attack, so Rankin's dissenting vote was seen only as a token voice of pacifism.

Rankin later investigated the possibility that President Roosevelt had actually taken steps to provoke the Japanese. During her investigation she received little help. Her findings were published in 1942 in the *Congressional Record*. Called "Some Questions About

Jeannette Rankin in 1968, presenting a petition calling for the end of the Vietnam War to her home-state senator, Senate majority leader Mike Mansfield

Pearl Harbor," the report tried to prove that Roosevelt had conspired with Britain's leader Winston Churchill to create a war between Japan and the United States. More than three decades later, Rankin's assertions were supported by British documents made public after the war that acknowledged Roosevelt's determination to get into World War II.

After her second term in Congress, Rankin decided not to run again. She was in her sixties and chose to continue her work for women's rights, peace, and disarmament as a civilian. Two decades later, when the Vietnam War was dividing the nation, Rankin became a spokesperson to end that war. She marched in protest, wrote letters, and gave speeches. Jeannette Rankin continued to work in the pursuit of peace until her death in 1973 at age ninety-two.

2 The Early Years

THE PASSAGE OF the Nineteenth Amendment and the tenure of Representative Jeannette Rankin publicized the notion that women could have a place in American politics if they chose. One might assume that getting the vote would have touched off a revolution for women. After women's suffrage succeeded in 1920, women did begin to vote in elections. But there were few who chose to run for office.

Was all Rankin's work and the fight for women's suffrage for naught? Absolutely not. Suffrage laid the foundation for full political participation by every American, male or female. But integrating women into the public framework of government was not easy. Social conventions still kept women from fully participating in their communities except in areas where it was felt a woman belonged. For instance, matters involving health care and children were felt to be women's issues. But having a woman direct men

Florence Kahn, Edith Nourse Rogers, and Mary Norton in 1925

in areas of economics and political thought seemed too hard to fathom. For many people, the difficulties of the day—getting work and feeding their families—took precedence over any issue of rights.

Still, there were many improvements in politics as a direct result of efforts by women in the 1920s and 1930s. They organized the League of Women Voters, a nonpartisan organization designed to promote political responsibility by providing information to voters and encouraging active participation in government. The League was an outgrowth of the National American Woman Suffrage Association. Women also organized the Joint Congressional Congress, tried to enter party offices, and ran for political offices.

During this period, many changes were occurring in American society. Because of a rise in industry in the 1920s, men, women, and children were needed to work in factories and mills. Many problems arose from the resulting economic changes. The number of women in the workforce was growing, but the jobs they held were not in the "public realm" or in high-paying professions. They were still not accepted into most professional training programs or universities to become doctors, lawyers, or merchants. Instead, they worked exhausting hours for little money on a factory line or in a sweatshop, or doing other menial labor that required little training. Their children often worked alongside them.

On October 29, 1929, the United States entered one of its darkest periods—The Great Depression. The stockmarket crashed, and in a matter of minutes personal and business fortunes were lost, industries were ruined, and millions of individuals were left with little hope. The following decade was a time of tremendous struggle for Americans. Food and unemployment lines grew while opportunity seemed nowhere to be found. The people turned to their leaders to see them through. Most notable was Franklin Delano Roosevelt, known as FDR. He was elected president in 1933 and held a tight reign on American politics until his death in 1945.

Women Legislators and the New Deal

Sworn into office along with FDR was a majority of "New Deal" Democrats. The president had promised his constituents "a new deal for America" and vowed to get people back to work. To do this, FDR pushed through a variety of laws that used public money to put people to work on public projects, such as building roads and dams. The New Deal Democrats were also very interested in developing social programs to help those in need. The welfare system and social security were developed during FDR's administration. His presidency was one of the first to put so much time and energy into addressing the basic human needs of the people. Issues women had been focusing on for years—working conditions, employment restrictions for women and children, health care for the poor—these were all taken up by Congress during FDR's tenure.

Before, during, and after the Depression, through the 1940s, women legislators found themselves in a Capitol that was less than welcoming and one that did not take them seriously. Indeed, many of the women in Congress during the first half of this century were there because of the "Widow's Mandate"—their husbands had died in office and the widows filled the seat for the remainder of the term. Party leaders often used widows to keep a seat occupied until they could put up a candidate of their choosing at the next election. Since it was assumed that a wife would vote as her husband would, the party felt safe that their interests would be protected. This alienation of women in

Congress was not due to partisan politics but rather to gender politics. Most men simply did not want to yield power to women.

Sometimes, though, the party leaders got a surprise. Many of the widows in Congress showed a penchant for politics and found a voice of their own. For these women, the option of running on their own names was an attractive one, and thus many political careers were born. Still, from Jeannette Rankin in 1917 to Willa Eslick (D–Tenn.; rep. 1932–33) in 1932, only fifteen women sat in Congress—and some of these woman didn't serve even a single day! They were appointed or elected at a time when Congress was not in session.

Changing the Debate

Imagine the vast change the country had to accept when women won the right to vote in national elections. For some people, it may have seemed that their worlds were turning upside down as women began to come out of the home, or the private realm, to take their place in the public domain.

As a group, women's interests were different from those of their male counterparts. Raising children, buying groceries, and managing a household were seen as women's work. What did men know of the price of bread or the care needed for a sick child? Perhaps this is one reason the women in Congress took up the fight of overworked and abused workers and took on child labor abuses. The attention to social issues, especially those directly affecting women and children, has been kept alive largely through the efforts of female legislators. Of course, men are just as concerned about the well-being of the people, but rarely did they make these issues a top item on their political agendas.

This is not to say that female members of Congress weren't interested in and knowledgeable about economic development, foreign affairs, and other, less tangible, political issues that came before the House. They were as talented and intelligent as their male colleagues, but they were judged by a completely different set of criteria.

As Ruth Baker Pratt noted from her time serving in the New York State Assembly, male politicians are judged as politicians, but women politicians are judged as women. Sixty years later, her thoughts still ring true. She once explained, "A man enters public life and not the slightest attention is paid to the fact that he is a man. A woman runs for office and there is more interest in the fact that she is a woman than in her qualifications for the job she seeks. . . . At every turn she is confronted with the fact that the activities of the world have been cut from a 'he' pattern."[1]

The 67th Congress in 1921–22 lists four women: Rebecca Felton in the Senate, and Winnifred Huck, Alice Mary Robertson, and Mae Ella Nolan in the House. Of these four women, Felton never truly served, and Representative Nolan couldn't wait to leave Washington and return to her quiet, stable life. Shortly after them, four more women who hadn't planned on lives in politics—Ruth Baker Pratt, Edith Nourse Rogers, Mary Norton, and Florence Kahn—rose to the occasion and made important contributions during careers that spanned decades.

Rebecca Felton: The First Female Senator

Although many regarded her appointment to the Senate as a farce, Rebecca Felton (Independent D–Georgia; sen. 1922) nonetheless recognized the opportunity to make an important statement. She said, "There are now no limitations upon the ambitions of women. They can be elected or appointed to any office in the land." These words, spoken in 1922, were received with either excitement or disdain from women across the country. It had been only two years since women in America won the right to vote in national elections, and Felton's appointment to fill a senatorial seat had really been just a grand political gesture. The governor of Georgia wanted to score a few points with the women in his state. But Rebecca Felton demonstrated great courage and determination in being recorded as the first female U.S. senator.

Georgia Governor Thomas W. Hardwick had dreams of going to the Senate himself. But in order to strengthen his base of support, he had to find a way to reach out to the women of his state, who had only recently been granted the right to vote. (Hardwick had voted against the Nineteenth Amendment.) At the same time, he had to tip his hat to the men of his state who were still stunned by the idea that women should have an equal voice in politics.

Governor Hardwick's opportunity came when the sitting senator, Thomas E. Watson, died with only a short time left in his term. As governor, Hardwick was responsible for naming someone to complete Watson's term. Since he planned to run for the seat himself in a few months, Hardwick thought he would "save" the seat by naming a woman to the post. That woman was Rebecca Felton, a well-known, outspoken advocate for women's rights and an active player in Georgia politics. Her husband, Dr. William Harrell Felton, ran for Congress as an Independent after the Civil War. Mrs. Felton joined her husband's campaign and remained a key advisor. She became his personal secretary—answering mail, keeping abreast on the issues that concerned him, and even editing his speeches. She was so involved

Rebecca Felton in 1922 at the wheel of her Ford

in her husband's congressional activities that many constituents looked upon her as their second representative.

Not everyone was pleased with this arrangement. After Rebecca Felton had published some articles under her own name, one newspaper editorial asked, "Which Felton Is the Congressman and Which the Wife?" After losing the next few elections, the Feltons began publishing a newspaper called the *Cartersville Free Press*. Rebecca Felton wrote unabashed columns deploring political corruption and stating her opinions on other issues of the day.

Dr. Felton eventually returned to public office, completing three terms in the Georgia state legislature. And his wife was with him every step of the way. When he died in 1909, Rebecca Felton continued her activism, joining the suffrage movement and speaking on issues of labor, education, and marriage laws. She was even invited to address the state legislature—the first woman to do so. Although not everyone agreed with her, Georgian politicians recognized Rebecca Felton as an intelligent, outspoken woman willing to work hard for her causes.

Governor Hardwick had wisely chosen a woman recognized by the state for her political contributions. At the press conference held to announce Felton's appointment, Hardwick also announced that he would be running for the seat in an election to be held in mid-October. The law read that as soon as a successor was elected, the appointed senator would be replaced. Since the Senate was not currently in session, and would not be until after the election, Rebecca Felton would never really be a senator.

It was no secret that Rebecca Felton would not really serve in the Senate. No one understood this better than Felton herself. But while Hardwick may not have intended for her name to actually be inscribed in the Senate rolls, she had other plans. She realized how meaningful it would be to have her name inscribed as the first female senator. Without letting anyone know her plans, she gracefully accepted the governor's offer.

Then, on November 20, 1922, for a completely unrelated matter, President Warren G. Harding chose to call a special session of Congress. This was the opportunity Felton needed to make her case. Her goal was to take the oath for the Senate. This would not be easy, because several senators had already announced that they would oppose admitting her. Remember, it was only two years since the women's suffrage amendment had even passed, so these men were not used to letting women vote, let alone serve in the Senate!

Undeterred, Felton boarded a train and on November 20 found herself standing before the United States Senate. One senator opposed her being sworn in on the basis of historic Senate rules, but he got no support from his colleagues. In fact, after being sworn in, Senator Felton received a rousing applause from the onlookers in the gallery as well as from the chamber of senators.

In her two full days sitting in the Senate, Felton did not have the opportunity to cast a vote. She did, however, seek to be recognized and said to the floor, "When the women of the country come in and sit with you, though there may be but a very few in the next few years, I pledge you that you will get ability, you will get integrity of purpose, you will get exalted patriotism, and you will get unstinted usefulness."[2]

Rebecca Felton foresaw the future with wonderful accuracy.

Winnifred Mason Huck

Like Rebecca Felton, many women in Congress didn't serve long enough to have left their stamp on legislation. Winnifred Mason Huck (R–Ill.; rep. 1922–23) won her seat in the House in a special election held in 1921 to fill the congressional term of her deceased father. There were only four months left in the term, leaving her little time to perform congressional duties. Still, she had a good deal to say.

Born into a political family in Illinois in 1882, Winnifred Mason was the daughter of William E.

Mason, a well-known and popular pacifist. She led an interesting and adventurous life. She never let society's mores stop her from pursuing her interests. As a journalist for a Chicago daily newspaper, Winnifred Huck once went undercover to investigate the effects of the prison system. Under an assumed name, she committed a crime and went to jail. After serving thirty days, she was released and spent months trying to get and keep jobs. Her experiences were publicized in speeches and in a series of newspaper articles.

Following in her father's footsteps, Representative Huck proposed a constitutional amendment requiring that a popular vote be held before the country could enter into war. The suggestion did not gain much support, but she had succeeded in making her opinions known.

In a lighter vein, Huck was the first female member of Congress to address the important question: Where was she to go to the bathroom?! Since Congress had always been all male, there were no female restrooms near chambers. Although the "Men Only" sign had been removed when Jeannette Rankin took office, the question of where women members could go to "powder their noses" remained unanswered.

Equality was an important issue for Representative Huck, who said that women differ from men only "as to what we believe to be the more important issues before our country." She articulated many of the goals that women had been striving to achieve:

> *We are anxious . . . that marriage shall not take away the woman's right to choose her own citizenship; that married women shall not be discriminated against in the economic world; and that the mother shall have in all states an equal right with the father in the care, custody, and control of the child. We want universal marriage and divorce law of the right sort. . . . Although we recognize the importance and absolute ne-*

cessity of appropriation and tariff bills, we feel that these other issues are equally important and should not be put off year after year.[3]

Unfortunately, because of her ill-timed career, Representative Huck was never able to introduce legislation to further her commitment to equality and women's rights.

Alice Mary Robertson

Surprisingly, not all women were in favor of suffrage. Many women saw politics as a dirty business, one in which women were too moral to dapple. This argument did not take self-destiny into account, but rather stayed mired in the teachings of the day: women were more moral and virtuous than men and they must do whatever it took to stay pure. This meant that women should not participate in the dirty worlds of politics and finance.

Alice Mary Robertson (R–Okla.; rep. 1921–23) was one of the women who believed such things, even though she was financially independent for much of her life and enjoyed a varied career. She felt that women had a certain place in this world and their moral superiority gave them special privileges. In her eyes, exchanging these privileges for the right to vote was not a good deal.

Despite her views on gender, she did "men's" work most of her life. She was born in 1854 to a white missionary family in what was then Oklahoma territory, an area designated for the resettlement of Native Americans driven from their traditional tribal homes. Alice Mary and her three siblings were raised to spread the gospel to their Indian neighbors. She attended Elmira College in New York, then returned to Oklahoma to become the first female clerk in the Indian Office of the Department of the Interior. She worked as an interpreter and stenographer at tribal peace negotiations in what was called Indian Territory. She also founded a school for Native American children, was a successful farm owner, and became an active supporter of the Spanish American War and World War I.

At the age of sixty-six, Robertson, affectionately called "Miss Alice," decided that "men have thrust the vote on us and now I am going to see whether they mean it."[4] So she ran for Congress. The newspapers refused to support her candidacy. For one thing, Oklahoma had a very strong Democratic presence and she ran on a Republican ticket. For another thing, the country was still coming to terms with the idea of women as political leaders.

Never deterred, Robertson took out small classified ads in the newspaper on a regular basis. Soon, everyone was picking up the paper each day to read what Miss Alice had to say. Her campaign slogan was "I cannot be bought, I cannot be sold, I cannot be intimidated." The tactic worked, and Ms. Robertson was elected to the 67th Congress in 1920. She meant what she said in her campaign slogan and was known for speaking her mind.

Very early on, Robertson established her style and met with contempt from women's groups around the country. Representative Robertson was not afraid to be unpopular. For example, she opposed the Sheppard-Towner bill, which was originally authored by Jeannette Rankin and established funds to help mothers and newborn infants. The cost of the bill was $1 million, excessive by Robertson's standards. Robertson also voted against the creation of the U.S. Department of Education because she thought that was too much government control in private lives, a theme that continues today in the Republican Party. This also had an impact on her views

Alice Mary Robertson in 1921

of integration. While she did not object to black and white children going to school together, she didn't think the federal government should force states to integrate schools.

Even with these views, Representative Robertson was a popular figure among many of her constituents, because she voted in favor of economic bills that would improve the state. She also enabled a veterans' hospital to be built. Aside from the real issues on her agenda, one of the publicity highlights of her two years in Congress was the opportunity to meet Lord and Lady Astor from Britain. At the time, Robertson was the only female member of the U.S. Congress and Lady Astor was the only female member of Britain's Parliament. Their photograph—the stunning and fashionable Lady Astor standing next to the serious and dour Representative Robertson dressed all in black—is a study of contrasts. Just because they were the same sex did not mean all women politicians were the same!

Robertson ran for reelection in 1922 but was voted out of office. She returned to Oklahoma and took on a variety of jobs. She wrote for the local newspaper and worked as a research assistant at the Oklahoma Historical Society. But the Depression seemed to rob her of much income, leaving her to depend on the generosity of friends and relatives. When she died of cancer in 1931, Alice Mary Robertson was remembered as "Oklahoma's Most Famous Woman."

Mae Nolan

Mae Ella Hunt Nolan (R–Calif.; rep. 1923–25) never wanted to be in politics. But when her husband, Johnny Nolan, died in 1923 just after winning reelection to Congress, the Republican leaders in his San Francisco district implored his wife to complete his term. Gracious and businesslike, Mrs. Nolan accepted the job and went to Washington.

Mae Hunt had met Johnny Nolan when he was first elected to Congress in 1912, and they were married soon after. Congressman Nolan had a reputation for being principled and for striving to help his constituents, many of whom were unskilled laborers working for less than a living wage. Mae Nolan tried to uphold his ideas during her term in Congress. With the help of her sister, who had been the congressman's secretary for several years, she worked hard to improve the lives of laborers. She was appointed to the Labor Committee, where she lobbied in support of her husband's bill to raise the minimum wage. She was also appointed to chair the House Expenditures in the Post Office Department Committee, the first woman to do so. The work on the Labor Committee, though, took precedence for her.

After her term in office, Congresswoman Nolan was ready to return to California, where she thought her young daughter could have a "normal home life" and where she could return to some of the leisure activities she had enjoyed before her husband's death. Mae Nolan was never called to a life in politics. Rather, she did her duty and, when she saw fit, returned to the life she had chosen.

Ruth Baker Pratt

Ruth Baker (R–N.Y.; rep. 1929–33) was born in 1877 into an affluent family. In 1903 her marriage to John Teele Pratt, a wealthy executive with the Standard Oil Company, made her welcome in New York's high society. In between social engagements, she managed a full staff of servants and raised five children.

She was very active in local Republican activities and rose up the party ranks. She was elected to one term in the New York Assembly (the first woman to do so), and did her best to combat the corruption peddled by Tammany Hall. Tammany Hall was the name given to the powerful Democratic machine that controlled most of New York's politics.

Pratt was outspoken, aggressive, and public in her tactics to combat the cigar-smoking men with whom she served. While she had not planned on seeking higher office, her efforts to reform New York politicians seemed fruitless. The voters supported her efforts, though, so she accepted a nomination to run for Congress in 1928. Her campaign office was jammed with volunteers, and she beat the favored Democratic opponent. Once in Congress, she was appointed to the important Banking and Currency Committee. Her tenure in Washington was distinguished by the many social gatherings she hosted as well as her skill in persuasion and her undying efforts on behalf of her constituents.

Representative Pratt's district covered the lights and glamour of Broadway, but a large part also included immigrants and working people who needed a voice in Congress. Pratt went out of her way to assist these people and "be their friend in Washington," as she sometimes said. She was an advocate for war veterans and always ready to assist constituents with individual problems, big or small, especially with immigration issues.

Pratt won reelection in 1930 but was defeated in 1932, the year the Democrats won House seats by a large majority on the coattails of FDR's New Deal. Even though she was not in Congress, Pratt did not stop her political and charitable work. She was involved with the Republican Party for most of her life. She also used her wealth and station to support many charitable and arts organizations, including the New York Philharmonic Orchestra.

Edith Nourse Rogers

When Edith Nourse Rogers (R–Mass.; rep. 1925–60) took her deceased husband's congressional seat in a special election in 1925, the pundits thought her stay in Washington would be brief. They couldn't have been more wrong! Edith Nourse Rogers has the distinction of serving in Congress longer than any other female member—from 1925 to 1960. For thirty-five years she was an unfailing source of support for veterans as well as for women across the country.

A Republican from Massachusetts, Representative Rogers usually voted along with her party. She is responsible for a number of bills that have shaped this country's history, especially on behalf of the military and veterans. She wrote legislation establishing a network of veterans' hospitals throughout America. She also saw to the formation of various women's organizations within the military, such as the navy WAVES (Women Accepted for Volunteer Emergency Service), the Marine Corps Women's Reserve, and the WAACs (Women's Army Auxiliary Corps), which was to attract 150,000 members.

Like Ruth Baker Pratt, Edith Nourse was born into a wealthy family and had no need to become involved in the inner workings of this country. But soon after her marriage to John Jacobs Rogers World War I began, and she worked for the American Red Cross and the YMCA caring for wounded soldiers. Back home, she traveled around the country visiting ill and disabled veterans and taking their complaints and concerns back to the White House.

Her wartime experiences never left her. In the House she introduced bills establishing pensions for widows of veterans. She was also a sponsor of the GI Bill of Rights, a collection of programs aimed at helping war veterans with education and health concerns.

Rogers also introduced a version of the Equal Rights Amendment in 1947. The men in power at that time saw that her bill never got out of the Judiciary Committee (the fate of many similar bills). During the 1950s Representative Rogers spoke out on issues of international concern. She originally supported the idea of the United Nations but then cautioned of the problems of admitting Communist China into its ranks. Her attention to the health and well-being of workers often occupied her time. She worked hard to promote the cotton industry and guard against falling wages in order to support the many mill workers in Massachusetts. Edith Rogers died at the age of eighty, just a few days before an election in which she was running unopposed.

Mary Teresa Hopkins Norton

A colleague of Representative Rogers in the 69th Congress in 1925 was Mary Teresa Hopkins Norton (D.–N.J.; rep. 1925–51), the first female Democratic Representative. Representative Norton was a tireless worker for social reform during the Depression in the 1930s, when Americans faced massive unemployment and personal strife. She was also a strong and fearless woman who took on battles in the House with confidence and parliamentary savvy. Her intelligence and talent helped pave the way for many of the women who followed in her footsteps.

Mary Hopkins was born to Irish immigrants who had settled in New Jersey. Only seventeen years old when her mother died, she took charge of the household. She became a stenographer, and in 1909, at the age of thirty-four, she married Robert Francis Norton, an old friend. After the death of her only child, Mary Norton threw herself into volunteer work for children's issues.

Like many women politicians, Norton entered politics after several years of community organizing. Most male politicians of this period had a professional background or started their career in politics without ever really getting involved at a community level. This may help explain the long-held assumption that male politicians would look after the money and female politicians would look after the people.

Mary Norton, though, proved to be adept at both. She captured the attention of a New Jersey Democratic political boss named Frank Hague. He was called "boss" because he controlled many of the Democratic politicians in the state and could make or break a career. Norton met Hague while seeking support for a charitable organization. He later asked her to lend her name to the Democratic State Committee. In 1922 she became the first woman elected as a New Jersey freeholder (state legislator).

Again at Frank Hague's urging, Norton ran for Congress and was elected in 1925. She became an even stronger leader and was the first woman to chair three committees: the District of Columbia Committee, the Labor Committee, and the Administration Committee. (In fact, only four other women have ever chaired even one House committee!)

Her unwavering efforts to improve government in Washington, D.C., won her many fans, but it was as chair of the Labor Committee that Representative Norton left her mark. Today, the Labor Committee is one of the most powerful and influential groups in Congress. But in 1937 it was just beginning to address the needs of America's workers. In Mary Norton, those workers had found a champion.

Robert Norton was supportive of his wife's career in politics, but his untimely death shortly after she entered Congress left Mary Norton a widow. She was able to throw herself entirely into the job, and she spent her twenty-six years in Congress working hard and focusing on the craft of politics. Her ability to pass crucial and often difficult legislation is legendary. For instance, she faced a very unfriendly Congress when she sought to pass FDR's Wage and Hours bill in the House. The bill basically set a minimum wage and a maximum working day for unskilled laborers, laws that we take for granted today.

In 1926 Mary Norton and Edith Nourse Rogers held a debate on radio about Republicans and Democrats in office.

Norton met with great resistance, tempered with anger and sexism, as the men of the House were not accustomed to listening to a woman. The bill failed the first time. But she was not afraid to use her powers to push it through. Undeterred, Mary Norton started over and got the bill passed on its second round through Congress.

In 1950 ill health reduced Norton to writing a note from a hospital saying she would not seek another term. After she regained her health, she worked with the Department of Labor. The last years of her life were spent in Connecticut, where she had moved to be near her sister.

She died in 1959 after an illustrious career in Congress that spanned three decades. Representative Norton was an important congressional player at a very difficult time in the country's history. She was also a pacesetter for the women who came after her. In fact, during her lifetime Mary Norton was so highly respected that she was even recommended as a Democratic nominee for vice president of the United States. She refused the honor, however, knowing that it would have been only a political ploy, since a majority of party voters were all ready to select a man to fill that spot.

Florence Prag Kahn

Smart, witty, confident—Florence Prag Kahn (R–Calif.; rep. 1925–37) was all of these. A San Francisco Republican who succeeded her deceased husband in Congress, she loved the spotlight and had a knack for politics. In fact, she was so well spoken, and so well liked by her constituency, that she served in Congress for twelve years. She was a respected member of the House and a skilled parliamentarian. She was even asked to preside over many debates on the House floor because of her ability to control members of Congress during sometimes heated arguments.

The daughter of Jewish immigrants, Florence Prag was a precocious child. She entered the University of California at age fourteen and, like her mother, became a teacher in a San Francisco high school. She then married an actor named Julius Kahn, and together they went to Washington. Julius was a Congressman representing a San Francisco district, and Florence served as his unpaid assistant. When Julius died in 1924, Florence was ready to assume his role. At first most people dismissed her as only a widow filling her husband's shoes. But it soon became clear that Florence Kahn had a mind of her own and an independent spirit. As she campaigned for reelection, her slogan was that she was pledged "to no man and to no thing"—a theme that has led many women's campaigns since.

When it came to following House rules, Representative Kahn also demonstrated a rare spirit by demanding a change in her committee assignment. The House leadership had assigned her to work on the Indian Affairs Committee. Since her district in San Francisco was not home to any Native Americans, she lobbied until they moved her to the Education Committee. Her goal was to sit on the Military Affairs Committee, which her late husband had chaired. Her persistence finally paid off.

During Kahn's third term in office, the party leadership made a stunning move and appointed her to the powerful Appropriations Committee—the one that decides where federal money gets allocated. Kahn was the first woman ever to sit on this committee.

This popular congresswoman became a great attraction. Spectators would sit in the House gallery waiting to hear what would come out of her mouth next. Florence Kahn was never at a loss for words. When asked why she was so popular, she replied teasingly, "Sex appeal." After her retirement from politics, when a reporter came to interview her, she said, "I know why you're here; you want to do my obituary." But when it came to the business of the country, Representative Kahn was anything but flip.

She was responsible for many important acts during her tenure. Most notably, she realized that in order for San Francisco to stay economically competitive it had to be better connected to the rest of California—literally. After much hard work, Representative Kahn received a unanimous vote from all the House members to appropriate $75 million to build the San Francisco Bay Bridge. The vote was a testament to her skills as a consensus builder and negotiator.

The years she served in Congress were between the two world wars, and America enjoyed a sense of peace, hoping never to relive the horrors of World War I. But Kahn didn't join the peace movement. Her credo was, "Preparedness never caused a war, unpreparedness never prevented one." She was also known as the "Mother of the FBI" because she crusaded for more funding of the Federal Bureau of Investigation when kidnapping was becoming an all-too-common crime. As a mother of two sons, she saw this appropriation as a guard against other mothers losing their children to kidnappers.

Never one to shy away from controversy, Florence Kahn fought for the causes she believed in without consideration of their popularity. She served in Congress until 1936, when she lost an election in which the Democrats swept the Republicans by a huge margin in the midst of the New Deal.

3

Family Connections

FOR SOME PEOPLE, politics is like the family business. Learning to negotiate its tricky waters is handed down from father and mother to son and daughter. Just as many congressmen's wives worked as their husbands' assistants (usually without a salary), daughters often assisted their politician fathers. Alice Roosevelt is one of the most famous political daughters. When her widowed father Theodore Roosevelt became president, Alice took on the duties usually assumed by the First Lady. It's said that "Miss Alice" was not only a popular hostess but also a woman with influence over her father.

Ruth Hanna McCormick, Ruth Bryan Owen, and Nancy Landon Kassebaum all followed in their fathers' footsteps to become members of Congress.

Ruth Bryan Owen (seated, right) with some of her family in 1925; this family photograph was the first since her mother (seated, left) became ill and an invalid and the last before the death of her father, William Jennings Bryan (left).

Lindy Boggs took her husband's place after he died in a plane crash and went on to build her own congressional career based on her own achievements. Her daughter, Cokie Roberts, did not become a politician, but she covers Capitol Hill as a reporter. She says proudly, "Politics is our family business." Frances Bolton took her husband's place in Congress and stayed on for almost three decades. She also served in Congress at the same time as her son.

Regardless of the exact relation, these women all found that they had a yearning and a talent for politics. None of them originally planned to have a career in Congress, but when the opportunity was thrust upon them, they found that they not only enjoyed it but excelled at it.

In some cases, the woman who followed her father's or husband's footsteps to a seat in Congress shared his ideas and beliefs on issues. Ruth McCormick agreed with her father, and Lindy Boggs worked alongside her husband to further their shared ideals. But for other women, such as Frances Bolton and Ruth Bryan Owen, personal opinions on the issues developed along with their political careers.

Ruth Hanna McCormick

Ruth Hanna McCormick (R–Ill.; rep. 1929–31) is remembered not for what she did while serving in Congress, but for her campaigns to get there. Ruth Hanna, the daughter of the Ohio business magnate and politician Marcus Hanna, enthusiastically studied politics at her father's knee. He was U.S. senator from 1897 to 1904 and a presidential contender until his death. If Senator Hanna was meeting with colleagues or planning his strategy for the next election, Ruth was right there at his side soaking up all the political knowledge available. And the knowledge was considerable.

Marcus Hanna was a self-made millionaire who sought a role for himself in leading the country—and the country's politicians. He was a strong force behind the election of President William McKinley, and he is still remembered as a driving force in the development of the Republican Party.

Ruth could not have had a more seasoned or politically astute teacher. With her marriage to Medill McCormick in 1903 (with President Theodore Roosevelt in attendance), her political education continued. The McCormick family of Chicago founded the prosperous International Harvester Company and the *Chicago Tribune* newspaper empire. In addition to being the wealthy heir to a fortune, Medill McCormick was becoming an influential player in American politics. In 1912, he was picked to manage Theodore Roosevelt's Midwest campaign office. That same year, he was elected to the Illinois State Legislature.

Ruth McCormick was involved in politics at every level. Her base was in grassroots groups—local community groups interested in particular issues. From her father she learned the lesson that Tip O'Neill would later explain as "all politics is local." Ruth McCormick was a genius at rallying popular support for candidates and causes. The support of so many voters helped her rise through the ranks of the Republican Party and helped her husband win his election to the Illinois State Legislature. They worked as a team on such issues as women's suffrage. Medill debated for it on the House floor while Ruth stumped for it in towns and cities throughout Illinois. Illinois granted women the right to vote in presidential elections in 1913, seven years before the Nineteenth Amendment made it a nationwide right.

Ruth McCormick's talent and experience made her instrumental in her husband's election to the House of Representatives and then to the Senate. She had looked at her role in politics as support for the men in her life, first for her father and then for her husband. But Medill McCormick died an untimely death in 1925. This event, and the success of suffrage, helped seal Ruth McCormick's fate. She began to look at politics with renewed interest for what she might accomplish as an officeholder.

The first step she took was to run for Republican Party national committeewoman. Democratic and Republican committeewomen and committeemen are elected by members of their party and have a great deal of power within the party at several levels of government. Ruth McCormick was told she would be a shoo-in for this post if she threw her support behind one of the gubernatorial candidates. But she refused, because she did not want to "owe" someone else in the party for her election, or have to seek approval for her every action within the party. The men who advised her did not realize the extent of her voter support or her political independence.

She ran for Congress in 1928 with the slogan, "No Promises and No Bunk." Her organizational skills assured her an overwhelming victory. At that time, there were nine women in Congress. Like most of them, Representative McCormick did not use the political jargon favored by the men. She spoke in everyday terms about the day-to-day issues facing the voters, rather than broad, impersonal topics like tariffs, isolationism, or economics. Her plain talk worked.

This victory was not enough to satisfy her. She had her sights set on the U.S. Senate. After only a month as a representative, McCormick waged a long and difficult battle for a Senate seat. She beat her opponent in the primary but lost a very public battle in the general election to a Democrat.

Despite her defeat, Ruth McCormick remained ac-

Ruth Hanna McCormick served on the House Naval Affairs Committee, shown here in 1930.

tive in politics and later married another Republican congressman, Albert G. Simms of New Mexico. But the Republican Party was overpowered by FDR and the New Deal, and she did not have an opportunity to run for public office again. She died in 1944.

Ruth Bryan Owen

William Jennings Bryan, the father of Ruth Bryan Owen (D–Fla.; rep. 1929–33), was called the "Great Commoner." He was a Democratic representative from Nebraska from 1890 to 1894. He ran for president three times, in 1896, 1900, and 1908, as the Democratic nominee. He lost to McKinley twice (in fact, he was defeated by the organizational skills of Ruth Hanna McCormick's father, Marcus Hanna, who oversaw McKinley's campaigns) and in his third bid he lost to William H. Taft. Nevertheless, Bryan was a champion of "populist" causes—always fighting for the underdog. He helped Woodrow Wilson win the Democratic nomination in 1912 and then served as Wilson's secretary of state.

Ruth Bryan admired both of her parents. Her mother was a law school graduate who had been admitted to the bar (not an easy feat for women in the first half of this century!). Ruth worked on her father's campaigns and assisted in his unsuccessful bids for the presidency. When she was only eighteen years old, she married William Homer Leavitt while they were both university students. They were divorced after only a few years, and Ruth was left to care for their two young children.

She began lecturing and writing to earn a living and proved to be very good at it. In 1910 she married Reginald Altham Owen, a British officer, and traveled the globe. Under a U.S. law of that time, she lost her own citizenship when she married a non-citizen. (Men did not lose their citizenship if they married non-citizens! Not until 1931 was a married woman's citizenship made fully independent from her husband's.) During World War I, Ruth Owen trained as a nurse and volunteered for American and British war efforts. After the war the family moved to Florida, where her husband died in 1927. Left to raise yet another son and daughter, Ruth returned to lecturing and was met by enthusiastic crowds. She was extremely involved in the community, chaired a number of different committees, and participated in a variety of organizations. Because of her involvement and her family history, it was not a far leap for her to consider running for office.

The challenge was to be successful as a woman candidate in Florida, a state that had voted *not* to ratify the Nineteenth Amendment. So it was almost a success when Ruth Owen lost her first bid for Congress by only 776 votes. She won her next attempt, in 1929, making her the first congresswoman from a Deep South state. Her district extended 500 miles (800 km) from Jacksonville to Key West.

Owen's four years in Congress were marked by her votes to support trade limitations and tariffs and her interest in environmental issues. Because of her efforts to protect the wilderness of Florida, the Everglades National Forest was created. She also took a great interest in young people and thought it was important to teach the next generation about civic duty and government. She led an annual tour of eighteen boys and eighteen girls from her district, showing them the White House and the original Constitution in the Library of Congress.

Ruth Owen's father was known for his social issues agenda. She, too, was concerned about social issues and fought for the development of programs for women and children. In her attempts to find information or services to help children, Representative Owen was forced to travel through a maze of disjointed public agencies and departments. It seemed to her that it would make sense to combine all the agencies. She proposed creating a federal Department of Home and Child. This proposal did not fare well with her congressional colleagues. They argued that such a department would be telling the states how to handle these issues, thus taking away the individual state's rights to govern.

This was 1931, though, and the health and wellbeing of children was still considered a woman's

Ruth Bryan Owen in 1932 greeting the new U.S. ambassador to England, Andrew Mellon

domain. Because of this attitude, it was thought that a woman would be appointed to lead this new department. Many congressmen did not like the idea of a woman being head of a department, because she would thereby hold a seat in the president's Cabinet.

Owen lost her third bid for Congress in 1932 because of her stand on prohibition; she was for a "dry" state where no alcohol could be legally available. For many people in the country at this time, a candidate's stand on prohibition was a defining characteristic.

Soon afterward, FDR appointed Owen as the United States minister to Denmark, the first woman to be appointed to such a high diplomatic position. While in Denmark she fell in love with and married Captain Börge Rohde. They returned to the United States, and President Harry Truman asked her to be a special assistant in the development of the United Nations in 1945. Four years later he named her as the alternative U.S. delegate to the UN General Assembly.

Ruth Bryan Owen's daughter, known as Rudd Owen, followed in her mother's footsteps and ran for Congress. She did not win, but even so, she confirmed that this family's political tradition was carried on by the daughters!

Frances Bolton

It would be an understatement to say that Frances Bolton (R-Ohio; rep. 1940–69) came from a political family. Her ancestors included Robert Treat Paine, who signed the Declaration of Independence, and the famous American patriot Thomas Paine. Her father was a U.S. senator, and her husband and son were both congressmen. Coming from an extremely wealthy family in Ohio, Frances Bolton wasn't expected to follow in her forefathers' footsteps. But she found she needed an outlet for her intelligence and her desire to help others.

At a young age, Frances Payne Bingham (the family changed the spelling of Paine to Payne) volunteered her time helping nurses visit tenements in Cleveland. The people she met and their living conditions, as well as the situations in which the visiting nurses labored, were forever etched into her mind. As a congresswoman, Frances Bolton would fight for nurses and the nursing profession.

Growing up in a rich family certainly had many

benefits. But her mother died early in Frances's life, and her father was not a demonstrative man so Frances felt somewhat alone. At an appropriate age Frances married Chester Bolton, a wealthy neighbor. They followed the prescribed rules of such families, and he eventually rose to become a congressman.

The Boltons moved to Washington, D.C., where Frances performed her social duties as a congressman's wife, and nursed her son back to health after he broke his neck in an accident. But more tragedy struck this family when Chester died in office. It was agreed that Mrs. Bolton would be put up as the candidate to fill her husband's unexpired term. No one thought such a "grand lady" would have much interest in the goings-on of Congress. But again the pundits were wrong. Frances Bolton won the seat by a very large margin and continued to represent her Ohio constituents for twenty-nine years.

It's interesting to note that Representative Bolton made many contributions to the legislative agenda of Congress. But the history books are fond of reminding us that she preferred the title "Congressman" to "Congresswoman." She said the word Congresswoman was not in the dictionary and therefore did not exist. She also preferred that her colleagues not refer to her as the "Gentlelady from Ohio," insisting instead on the term "Gentlewoman." The semantics of Congress can be very important, and this distinction was not lost on Representative Bolton.

Even as she was working to be treated on an equal basis with her male colleagues, Representative Bolton strove to teach the other female members of the House what was appropriate in attire and action—and what was not! For instance, she is said to have warned members about wearing hair curlers or chewing gum on the House floor.

During her years in public service, Representative

Frances Bolton and other members of the House and Senate Foreign Relations Committees watch in 1950 as President Harry S. Truman signs into law a bill authorizing $3.25 billion for foreign aid.

Bolton was very generous with her money. As Chair of the Foreign Services Committee and its ranking minority member, Bolton often paid for official trips out of her own funds rather than spend the taxpayer's money. And she took a great many trips. Representative Bolton believed in learning about a situation firsthand, much as she learned about nursing and the trials of being poor in this country, and she often led delegations on fact-finding missions to other countries. Some of these trips occurred during wartime, but the danger did not deter her.

Bolton also used an inheritance to establish the Payne Foundation. It was through this foundation that Mrs. Bolton found an additional outlet to help develop nursing schools and training programs for women.

While she would never be described as a liberal, Mrs. Bolton earned a reputation for treating everyone equally—and expecting others to do the same. This applied to men and women (she thought women should be drafted, too, to defend our country) and to whites and blacks.

In 1957, Bolton went into the history books. Her son Oliver ran for a congressional seat, and they became the only mother-and-son team to serve concurrent terms. They didn't always agree on the issues, and it was almost a relief for her when her son decided not to seek another term.

When Cleveland's congressional districts were redrawn in 1968, Bolton could not beat her opponent, Charles Vanik, another long-serving congressman. He moved into her district to challenge her and won. After so many years in Washington, Frances Bolton rejected the offer to become a diplomat; at the age of eighty-three, she was finally content to retire.

Lindy Boggs

The Boggs are a political family, there's no two ways about it. Congressman Hale Boggs was a respected member of the House for years. His wife, Corinne Boggs, known as Lindy (D–La.; rep. 1973–91), was a partner with her husband. She was intimately involved in her husband's political activities, and it was known and appreciated that they worked as a team. When Congressman Boggs's plane disappeared during a 1972 campaign, it came as no surprise that Lindy Boggs received the support of the Louisiana Democratic Party leaders to take his place. Not only that, but she also kept their support and continued to win elections from her district.

Lindy Boggs was well versed in party politics and knew how to get things done in Washington. She joined the Congresswomen's Caucus in its infancy (see Chapter 6), and she also had the respect of her male colleagues. This meant she could fight for the issues important to women and still retain good working relationships with the men. During the time Boggs served, women were just beginning to crack the glass ceiling that separated them from leadership roles in Congress. Because the Democrats controlled Congress in the early 1970s, they felt they had more room to promote some of their women members without losing power. Lindy Boggs benefited and was appointed to the Executive Subcommittee of the Democratic Caucus. She served there from 1979 to 1982.

Her daughter, Cokie Boggs Roberts, is a well-known political commentator specializing in the business of Congress for National Public Radio and network television. Cokie Roberts learned about the world of politics not just from her parents but also from the vantage point of a nonpartisan reporter. Her views of women in Congress are well founded. In a 1990 speech, Roberts told a college graduating class that "the women of America should basically be on their knees to the women in Congress of both political parties."[1] She pointed out that it is the women in Congress who continue to force discussion on such social

Corinne "Lindy" Boggs was sworn in to the House to succeed her late husband in 1973.

issues as child-support enforcement, day care, equal credit, and domestic violence. History agrees that it has been the women members of the House and Senate who write bills and fight for the passage of laws that have a direct effect on the lives of women and children.

To accomplish their tasks, congresswomen have had to learn how to get things done in Washington. Although many learned these lessons early from the experience of their fathers or husbands, each congresswoman has had to develop a style of her own. And even with the name recognition and polite courtesies that come from being in a politically connected family, they have had to learn how to win the respect of their male colleagues. Some, like Senator Margaret Chase Smith, earned the respect of the entire country.

Margaret Chase Smith

MARGARET CHASE SMITH (R–Maine; rep. 1940–49, sen. 1949–73) was a woman of promise—and of promises. During her thirty-two years in both houses of Congress she developed a well-deserved reputation for keeping her word. This reputation held her in good stead. The voters of Maine continued to return her to Washington where, as a senator, Margaret Smith held the highest leadership position ever attained by a woman in Congress, before or since. As chair of the Senate Republican Conference, she helped plan party strategy and enjoyed an influential voice in determining committee assignments.

Because Smith served in the Senate for twenty-four years, she was also entitled to many of the perks that come with seniority. In addition to her work on the Armed Forces Committee, Senator Smith enjoyed other influential posts, including the

Margaret Chase Smith on Edward R. Murrow's television show See It Now *in the 1950s.*

Appropriations, Government Operations, and Rules committees.

All of this from a woman who refused the pomp and circumstance accorded to senators and relied instead on old-fashioned hard work and attendance. (Her record for being in attendance for consecutive roll-call voting still stands.)

Involved in politics since her twenties, Margaret Chase became Somerset County Republican Committeewoman in 1928. A few years later she married Clyde Harold Smith, a man twenty-two years her senior. Mr. Smith was no political novice. He had held a series of state offices, and in 1936 he went to Congress as one of the few GOP ("Grand Old Party," a nickname for the Republican Party) representatives in a sea of FDR Democrats.

Margaret Smith went to Washington with her husband and became his secretary (paid) as well as his eyes and ears on a number of fronts. It was Margaret Smith (she disliked being called Mrs. Smith) who often returned home to Maine to meet with constituents, and it was Margaret Smith, not Clyde Smith, who traveled to different states collecting facts and figures for his work on the prestigious Labor Committee.

Not long before the 1940 elections, Clyde Smith suffered a heart attack and was warned that the stress of a campaign would further damage his health. The Smiths decided that Margaret would file for the election, and Clyde would take her place when he felt better. That plan was foiled when, in April 1940, Representative Smith suffered another heart attack and died. Margaret Smith was voted in easily in a special election to fill her husband's seat, and then she won the regular election for a full term. It wasn't just the state party leadership that endorsed her candidacy; her work with various grassroots organizations and coalitions helped her enormously when it came time to get votes.

In the House of Representatives

Once in Congress, Smith was denied her husband's place on the Labor Committee and assigned to less influential committees—a fate met by most women representatives. But Representative Smith did not make any grand gestures to get reassigned. Rather, she went about her business and did the best job possible on the assignments she was given. Margaret Smith had plans to be in politics for a long time and was a believer in working one's way up the ladder. And climb up the ladder she did.

In 1943, after several years of lobbying party leaders, she was finally assigned to the Naval Affairs Committee. As a member of this committee she could help Maine's economy grow; Naval Affairs oversaw the shipbuilding and naval activities vital to Maine's economic health. During this period, she introduced legislation to create the WAVES—Women Accepted for Voluntary Emergency Service. WAVES essentially took over non-fighting jobs during wartime to free men for military duties. This wasn't the first time the idea had been presented. The WAACs—Women's Auxiliary Army Corps—had been in existence for many years. But Smith, along with Representative Edith Nourse Rogers, fought for women to be allowed to work in hospitals and offices overseas.

The WAVES program was not without opposition. In 1941, even though the country was embroiled in World War II, women were assumed to be too delicate to participate in men's wars. Male congressmen balked at the idea. As one said, "There will be hardships that no American woman should have to endure." Without skipping a beat, Smith replied, "Then we'd better bring all the nurses home." Of course, women have served in support positions during every war in which America fought. In the Civil War, World War I, World War II , Korea, and Vietnam, women were an integral support to the fighting forces. The WAVES soon became a valued force in World War II.

Although she unequivocally supported women's rights, Smith said, and maintained, "If there is one thing I have attempted to avoid it is being a feminist. I definitely resent being called a feminist."[1] She did not feel she should be accorded special privileges because she was a woman. She also said the only reason more women were not in politics was because they chose not to try. Her actions in many areas, however, tell us that Smith was indeed a very strong advocate of women's rights. In 1945 Smith and Rogers again joined forces, becoming the first female representatives to add their names to the Equal Rights Amendment. (This amendment, which would have granted equal rights regardless of gender, has traveled through deep and murky waters for many decades. Although Congress finally approved it in 1972, it was never ratified by enough states and thus is not part of our Constitution.)

Pinch-Penny Campaigns

Margaret Chase Smith had to win a great many campaigns to serve in Congress for so many years. But she won each race with a minimal amount of money and no paid campaign staff. In today's campaigns it seems as if the candidate with the most money to spend will be the winner. In the 1950s and 1960s, campaign money, while not such an issue as it is today, was very important. Nevertheless, Smith held herself to very high standards as a representative and senator, refusing to spend public or private money to win a race. She felt that taking large sums of money from people or organizations would make her beholden to their views and wishes. She also never compromised her work in Congress—she returned home to Maine to campaign only on weekends or when Congress was not in session.

Representative Smith had dreams of moving to the Senate, as did many representatives. A great opportunity for this arose in 1948, when one of Maine's senators was retiring. Because the state was solidly Republican, Smith knew that her battle would be in the primary election, where she would be up against some of the GOP's strongest and smartest male candidates. Not many people thought she stood much of a chance. One politician said, "This little lady has simply stepped out of her class."[2] But once the campaign got underway, she proved him wrong.

Representative Smith was determined to keep her roll-call attendance record going while campaigning, and to attend to all the business of being a representative. Since she had no paid campaign staff she relied on a battalion of volunteers. In the 1940s, travel from Washington to Maine was more difficult than it is today. The plane ride was long and there were no direct flights.

During one campaign trip, Smith arrived in Maine to find icy roads and the heavy snows of winter. She slipped on a patch of ice and injured her arm. Just a few hours later, with her arm in a sling, she appeared at a campaign event and was immediately compared with the other candidates, who were all male, all healthy. None of the men, though, appeared as tough as the woman who was hurt but still showed up to speak. As you might imagine, this won her a lot of support.

Her overall campaigns were far from the professional, well-orchestrated efforts of her opponents. Smith reminded the voters of her accomplishments in the House of Representatives and spoke with them on their own terms, in a very down-to-earth manner. Like the hare and the turtle, the other GOP candi-

Margaret Chase Smith was the only senator among the seventeen women in the 84th Congress. She posed in 1955 on the House steps of the capitol with the female representatives (left to right): Edith Nourse Rogers, Cecil M. Harden, Marguerite Stitt Church, Mary Elizabeth Farrington, Elizabeth Kee, Edith Green, Martha W. Griffiths, Senator Smith, Frances Bolton, Katharine St. George, Edna F. Kelly, Gracie Pfost, Coya Knutson, Ruth Thompson, Leonor K. Sullivan, Vera Buchanan, and Iris Faircloth Blitch.

dates didn't pay much attention to this woman candidate who drove her own car and campaigned only on weekends. They didn't notice that Margaret Smith had won voters across the state. When primary day came, she racked up more votes than all of the other candidates combined! She went on to win the general election handily.

Speaking Her Conscience

As in her first years in the House, Senator Smith was given relatively unimportant committee assignments. Again she persevered, worked hard, and won the respect of the men with whom she shared the title Senator. What they didn't share with her was the courage to speak out against wrongdoing.

Accustomed to speaking out when she saw a wrong, Senator Smith was the first Republican to publicly lash out against Senator Joseph McCarthy, a Republican from Wisconsin. It was 1950, in the midst of "McCarthyism," when the congressional House Un-American Activities Committee (HUAC) was wreaking havoc in the country. In public hearings held under McCarthy's direction, American citizens were accused of participating in Communist activities and pressured to give the names of friends and coworkers who were also suspected of being Communists.

Many, many lives were ruined and reputations damaged by Senator McCarthy and his cohorts. The fear of Communism was so deeply ingrained in so many people that no one was willing to contest McCarthy's growing power. His fellow senators saw his increasing popularity and decided to keep quiet, regardless of their true feelings. Many even tried to ride on McCarthy's coattails to share in the publicity.

It may be hard to imagine now, but the tide of fear that had overtaken the country was so powerful that even President Dwight Eisenhower did nothing to stop McCarthy. Some senators actually helped the effort privately. At one point, McCarthy was made chairman of the Government Operations Committee, even though he was not a senior member of the Senate. Smith also served on this committee, and McCarthy immediately took action to dissolve her of any real power. One high-ranking senator could have intervened on her behalf, but he chose not to. It was as if an evil force had taken over the Senate—and the country. No one had the courage to stand up to McCarthy.

With a famous speech and a written statement signed by six other senators, Smith rebuked Joe McCarthy for abusing the power and authority of the Senate and rebuked the Senate as a whole for standing aside and allowing such abuse to occur. This was a gutsy thing to do, because the Senate is noted for its intricate rules and regulations, many of which have to do with respecting fellow senators. A member of that body cannot call a colleague ugly names or resort to other childish tactics without risking the ire of the entire Senate.

Smith's famous "Declaration of Conscience" was delivered on June 1, 1950, when she had been a senator for only one year in an institution that accords power based on seniority. She said:

> *It is ironical that we senators can debate in the Senate, directly or indirectly, by any form of words impute to any American, who is not a senator, any conduct or motive unworthy, or unbecoming an American—and without that non-senator American having any legal redress against us—yet if we say the same thing in the Senate about our colleagues we can be stopped on the grounds of being out of order. . . . As a United States senator, I am not proud of the way in which the Senate has been made a publicity platform for irresponsible sensationalism. I am not proud of the reckless aban-*

don in which unproved charges have been hurled from this side of the aisle.[3]

The difficulties between McCarthy and Smith grew personal. When asked why he didn't respond directly to her accusations, McCarthy shook off the charge by saying he didn't "fight with women senators." In further attempts to discredit her, he began to make jokes about "Snow White and the six dwarfs" and accused one of the male senators who signed the Declaration of "speaking through a petticoat."[4]

But McCarthy's bravado in the face of Senator Smith's charges did not sustain his political career. It took some time, but Senator Joe McCarthy was finally brought down, and Senator Smith played a key role. McCarthy had backed a candidate to run against Smith in the 1954 Republican primary. He even traveled to Maine to campaign for his candidate and against Smith. But Smith won by a five to one margin. This overwhelming victory proved that Joe McCarthy was not invincible, as many had believed. His hold on America was beginning to weaken, and Senator Smith knew it.

Not long after the election, the Senate moved to censure McCarthy for his conduct during and after the HUAC hearings. McCarthy eventually lost all of his power and influence, and he remains a sinister figure in American history.

Reading the Declaration of Conscience and publicly denouncing McCarthy may have been a defining moment for Senator Smith. But what many people now remember Margaret Chase Smith for was her bid for the presidency in 1964. Much of the press dismissed her attempts to reach the White House. One news magazine called her decision to run "frivolously feminine."[5] But many of the voters and her colleagues did take her seriously.

At the GOP National Convention, where delegates

chose the party's candidate for president, Smith was nominated by Vermont Senator George Aiken. Representative Frances Bolton and others gave seconding speeches. With these speeches, Margaret Chase Smith became the first woman ever nominated for president by a major political party. She received twenty-seven delegate votes. Only the GOP's final choice, Barry Goldwater, received more votes than Smith.

Throughout her many years fighting for justice in Congress, Senator Smith never lost her sense of humor. An often-related story has a reporter asking her during Harry Truman's presidency what she would do if she woke up one morning in the White House. She answered, "I'd go straight to Mrs. Truman and apologize. Then I'd go home."[6]

After her bid for the presidency, Smith returned her attention to the Senate and to developing the Republican Party. As chair of the Senate Republican Conference, Smith again broke through barriers—she was the first woman to attain such a high post within a major political party. She presided over party caucuses (meetings) and helped determine committee assignments and strategies.

Although loyal to her party, Margaret Smith voted and spoke her conscience. If this meant voting with Democrats, so be it. Many women in Congress have retained their independence in voting. Jeannette Rankin, Shirley Chisholm, Nancy Kassebaum—all of these women reserved the right to vote as they saw fit on a particular issue, regardless of the directives from party leaders. While such independence is often rewarded at the ballot box, it is usually punished within the politics and dealmaking of Congress.

Margaret Chase Smith was finally defeated in a 1972 election when a Democrat, William D. Hathaway, defeated her attempt at a fifth Senate term. She returned to Maine and joined the Woodrow Wilson

Margaret Chase Smith in 1964 announcing her candidacy for the Republican presidential nomination

Foundation as a traveling scholar, visiting eight different colleges. She also joined the board of directors of several companies and organizations, such as the Lilly Endowment and the U.S. Supreme Court Historical Society.

She began an association with the Northwood Institute, a business management college, and eventually donated her Skowhegan, Maine, house and its 15 acres (6 ha) to the college.

Senator Smith became ill in 1990 and suffered a debilitating stroke five years later. She died on May 29, 1995, in her home in Skowhegan. She was ninety-seven years old.

5

Decades of Change

THE 1960S AND 1970s were a time of revolution and rebellion in America. Civil rights, feminism, gay and lesbian rights—all of these movements were fueled by the energy from protests against the Vietnam War. Women were ready to take another step out of the private home and into the public arena. Feminism was enjoying a "second wave" as women from different classes struggled to redefine themselves and their futures. (The "first wave" of feminism began in the 1800s when Elizabeth Cady Stanton and Susan B. Anthony began the long fight for women's suffrage.) There were huge protest marches in Washington, D.C., and New York City; "consciousness raising" sessions where women shared their most personal thoughts and feelings; and rebellions on very

Six of the twelve female Democrats who served in the House in 1973 (left to right): Martha W. Griffiths, Shirley Chisholm, Elizabeth Holtzman, Barbara Jordan, Yvonne Brathwaite Burke, and Bella Abzug

personal levels. Behind the slogan "The Personal is Political," women were beginning to realize that rebellion comes in many forms. Even for a wife to announce to her husband that she would no longer guarantee dinner on the table each night at five could be a political act.

Integrated into this were many small social movements, often supported by the work of women. Grassroots organizations swirled together into a powerful force reinvigorating a generation. Many observers credit President John F. Kennedy, who defeated Richard M. Nixon in 1960, with spurring a new sense of political participation. He inspired individuals to responsible action with his inaugural address in 1960, in which he urged, "Ask not what your country can do for you—ask what you can do for your country." He put a public face on a broad-based network of thousands of women and men across the country, across ethnic, racial and gender lines, who were working toward liberation and equality.

This social and political upheaval propelled America to take another look at itself, to analyze the notions it had always held so dear. Notions of gender stereotyping and limited opportunities open to women were discussed in newspaper editorials, over dinner tables, and at organizational meetings and rallies. But like women's work in the earlier part of the century, the political groups being organized benefited greatly from women behind the scenes who did the grunt work, collected money, and pounded the pavement for signatures, support, and votes. Often it was men who benefited in the public eye. They were the ones who won elections or rose to executive leadership positions.

This was a lesson not lost on the women involved. Shirley Chisholm was tired of always working for male candidates, black and white, in races for Congress or the New York State Assembly. In 1964 she seized the chance to run for a state assembly seat for herself. Bella Abzug also chose to run herself rather than support another in a string of male candidates.

John F. Kennedy did help generate an interest in politics, both local and national. The theme of his administration was characterized as "Camelot," from the famed King Arthur tales. Camelot was an imaginary place where all the knights were considered equal when it came to finding a place at the round table. (This image actually came from a reference used by Jacqueline Kennedy after JFK's death.) Also, "a place at the table" is a widely used metaphor describing the inclusion of people when it comes to deciding and discussing issues. Having a place at the table means you and your concerns are represented.

The growth of grassroots reforms in civil rights and feminism reflected continuing strains in America's social fabric. The reality was that racism was rampant and far from subtle. Sexism was so institutionalized that it took years before women in the feminist movement could even identify and articulate some of the underlying problems. Whether inspired by Kennedy, by anti-war protests, or by other public issues, millions of Americans were drawn to participate in the political system. For the first time, thousands of women found their way into mid-level positions in party politics and grassroots political organizations.

Even in this time of change, though, the number of women in Congress actually diminished from a peak of nineteen in 1961 to only eleven in 1969. Many women were finding positions of political power, but at state and local levels. Shirley Chisholm was elected to the New York State Assembly (the first African-American woman to accomplish this). Dianne Feinstein was a vocal member of the San Francisco Board of Supervisors and later that city's mayor. Barbara Jordan was elected to the Texas State Legislature. These women continued to overcome obstacles to their advancement. They entered national politics in the 1960s—along with the likes of Patsy Mink, Bella Abzug, and Pat Schroeder—and earned a new level of respect from colleagues and constituents.

Patsy Mink

During the 1960s and 1970s it seemed as if the doors to public life had swung open to women. Law schools and medical schools were reforming their discriminatory policies against women. Situation comedies on television portrayed the life of the working woman with characters like Mary Tyler Moore's Mary Richards and Marlo Thomas's "That Girl." But the truth of the matter was faced by women like Patsy Mink (D–Hawaii; rep. 1965–77; 1990–). She broke through many of the barriers women faced, but her persistence was tested over and over again throughout her career in politics.

Patsy Takemoto was born in a small village on the island of Maui in 1927. Although she originally began studying medicine and earned a degree in zoology and chemistry, she decided on a career in law in her search for independence. She married John Mink, a geologist, and he has continually supported her political career.

After receiving her law degree from the esteemed University of Chicago Law School in the early 1950s, Mink returned to Hawaii to find a job with an established law firm. She was told she should stay home and raise babies, not practice law. Incensed, Mink opened up her own practice. At the same time, she became involved with the Democratic Party and Hawaii's attempts to win statehood. (Hawaii was then considered a territory; it did not gain statehood until

President Lyndon Johnson greets Patsy Mink at a White House reception for new members of Congress in 1964.

1959.) Although Hawaiians were considered Americans, they had no representation in Congress.

Patsy Mink had studied on the mainland and so enjoyed a broad perspective of American politics. The Republican Party dominated Hawaiian politics, but Mink brought a new Democratic outlook. She was instrumental in forming a group called the Young Democrats. This group promoted Democratic candidates for elected positions and was very successful in bids to gain seats in the Hawaiian legislature.

In 1957, after developing strong relationships within the national Democratic Party, Mink decided to run for a seat in what was then called the Territory of Hawaii's House of Representatives. She served in that body for one term. Then she was elected to the Hawaii Senate, where she served two terms.

When Hawaii became a state in 1959, a seat in the U.S. House of Representatives opened. Mink mounted a bid for this seat and lost. Undeterred, she regained her state senate seat and then ran again for Congress in 1964. This time she won.

When the Mink family moved to Washington, D.C., so that Patsy could begin serving her congressional term, the war in Vietnam was heating up and President Lyndon Johnson was committing more troops to the effort. Like most women in Congress at that time, Mink was decidedly antiwar. Proud of her Asian heritage, she reminded her constituents back home that there were racial overtones prevalent in the Vietnam War and that "Asians should not be killing Asians."

With her particular antiwar stance, Mink ran into a common problem in politics—the collision of social concerns with economic worries. Although many people in Hawaii probably agreed that the war was wrong, the state was home to a number of military installations. The war increased the activity of these installations and boosted Hawaii's economy. Nevertheless, Representative Mink held true to her convictions and continued to oppose the war.

She was not alone in this opposition. Over the course of about ten years, most of the other women in Congress also made strong antiwar speeches and introduced numerous bills to end the conflict. Shirley Chisholm's maiden speech (the first speech given on the House floor by a new congressmember), for example, was a virulent anti-Vietnam War plea. Many of her colleagues immediately labeled her a trouble-maker, something she would hear often in her political career.

Representative Mink is known for sticking with her convictions no matter what the political tide may bring in. She has served in the House of Representatives (although not continuously) for more than ten years and has developed and championed a string of issues. These range from education to environmental protection of Hawaii's vast natural resources to labor relations to equal rights for women and minorities.

Mink was a strong supporter of a very important amendment called Title IX of the Education Amendment Act of 1972. As she said, it was important to add "those three little words" to the amendment so it would say that opportunities for education cannot be denied "because of sex." On the college level, Title IX assured women a place on university rosters. The amendment passed, but it remains controversial today because it is still a struggle to assure female students the same opportunities as male students—in the classroom, in sports programs, and in the job market.

Congresswoman Martha Griffiths (D–Mich.; rep. 1955–75) recalled that her husband was accepted to Harvard Law School in the late 1930s, but she was denied because Harvard did not even consider accepting women. The Griffiths chose instead to attend the University of Michigan Law School and graduated together. Congresswoman Pat Schroeder, who was accepted to Harvard Law School in the 1960s, recalls being yelled at by male classmates for "taking a man's place." Such instances have been drastically reduced because of Title IX and Representative Mink's heroic efforts to get it passed.

Between her congressional terms Mink has served as Assistant Secretary of State for Oceans and International, Environmental and Scientific Affairs under President Jimmy Carter; president of Americans for Democratic Action; and chair of the Honolulu City Council. She was also a professor at the University of Hawaii. She is a past member of the National Women's Law Center's board of directors and of the Public Citizen's board of directors, a national public consumer protection interest group.

Upon her return to Congress in 1990, Representative Mink was untiring in her support of bills and programs that make life easier and more fair for men and women alike. She supported the Family and Medical Leave Act, which ensures that an employee may take leave from work to care for a newborn child or an ailing family member without fear of losing her/his job. Civil rights, fairness in the workplace, and the equality of women have remained high on her social issues agenda.

Mink represents a unique state, and many concerns specific to Hawaii consume her time. The first is that Hawaii is about 5,000 miles (8,000 km) away from Washington, D.C. As you can imagine, this limits a representative's opportunities to return home and meet face-to-face with constituents. To overcome the distance, Representative Mink manages to stay in touch through regular mailings and trips home whenever possible.

It is a struggle to preserve Hawaii's natural beauty and to sustain its agricultural industries. Representative Mink helped bring to fruition the Kaloko-Honokohau National Historical Park, which was approved by Congress in 1972. She is also a vocal supporter of industry in her district and is always looking out for the interests of the sugar and nut farmers in the rural areas she represents.

Because Hawaii is truly a melting pot of different nationalities and racial backgrounds, Mink's constituents have often needed her help on immigration issues. For instance, she found that tight immigration laws and visa restrictions meant that citizens of some countries experience more difficulty in receiving approval to enter the United States than those from other countries. Although this problem is not unique to Hawaii, Mink introduced legislation to standardize and expedite the cumbersome process of permitting family members to enter the country for visits or even for family funerals.

Some of Representative Mink's most heartfelt actions have come from her efforts at raising the voices of women and raising the standards of women in this country. She was one of the congresswomen who stormed the Senate Judiciary Committee to ensure that Anita Hill was heard during Clarence Thomas's Supreme Court confirmation hearings in 1991. She was also outspoken during the Operation Desert Storm conflict with Iraq.

After the congratulations for Desert Storm were long forgotten, the true picture of the American military came to light in 1992 when two scandals were made public. The first was that even though women were making great strides in the armed forces, they were far from equal; during the Desert Storm conflict, some women were even raped and molested by their fellow *American* soldiers. The second scandal was the Tailhook Convention. At an officially sanctioned annual gathering of navy pilots, military and civilian women were molested by drunken male pilots.

To Mink, Desert Storm reflected the general issue of women's role in the military. She said, "What comes up in people's minds is how badly women were treated over there. Even if we get into another military mess, that issue [equity for women] will become even more intense. . . . The whole environment has been very profoundly changed."[1] In part because of the support and vocal outcry of women in Congress, women in the military and in other facets of life are willing to come forward. Two examples are the female lieutenant who brought the Tailhook Convention to light and the testimony of Anita Hill at the Clarence Thomas hearings. But you can be sure that women across the country are finding their voices.

When it comes to women in politics, Representative Mink is firm in her stance that no obstacle is too big to overcome. As she put it:

> *The key, the only thing that counts, is whether a woman is genuinely dedicated to the ideal of doing something that will make a difference to her community and to her country. If she has this drive, if she's convinced she can make a contribution, if she's serious and has worked hard and shown the ability to take positions and to stand behind them, to fight for her beliefs, then she cannot fail at an election.*[2]

Shirley Chisholm

The political career of Shirley Chisholm (D–N.Y.; rep. 1969–80) proves Mink's point. As a college student, young Shirley St. Hill was passionate about politics and yearned to participate in political debate and discussion. She learned this from her father. As a girl, Shirley eavesdropped on her father's discussions with fellow Caribbean immigrants and listened to their talk of civil rights.

Shirley Chisholm is an ambitious woman who was born to immigrant parents from Barbados. They and her grandmother instilled in her a strong sense of pride and the importance of education. Chisholm learned these lessons well. After graduating from Brooklyn College and spending the first part of her career in education, Chisholm wanted to take these lessons to Washington. She always had an interest in politics but was told those doors were closed to her.

While there was some opportunity for involvement, Chisholm mostly remembers being relegated to women's committees and background work. During her twenties she began to attend the meetings of the Democratic clubs in her area of Brooklyn, New York. The city of New York was ruled by the Democratic Party in those days, and if you wanted anything—from garbage pickup to better schools—you went to the Democrats. For years, Shirley Chisholm paid her dues working for the Democrats. But at the same time she was always pushing the limit of "acceptability." When she was told to work with the other "ladies" on the annual fund-raiser to raise money for the men's activities, Chisholm demanded that they be given a budget from the club coffers. And when she went to a segregated meeting with black people seated on one side of the aisle and white people on the other, Chisholm sat right in front on the "white" side. But she was adamant that racism was not her biggest obstacle. "I've suffered worse discrimination as a woman than as a black," she once said.

This was true from her first election to the New York State Assembly to her historic run for the Democratic presidential nomination in 1972. When the chance to run for the state assembly arose, Chisholm grasped for it hungrily. After years of working for the men, it was now her turn. If she succeeded—and no one thought she would—she would become the first African-American woman to represent a district in the New York state legislature. Chisholm was already known as a troublemaker, and this endeavor only confirmed it. She was seen as "out of her realm" by both men and women alike. Her political challengers used pressure tactics and told the voters that politics was a "man's job." Yet behind those men in politics lay the work of women like Chisholm! Their canvassing and vote-getting was what got those men elected, year after year, to positions of political power.

Like Patsy Mink, Shirley Chisholm had a very supportive husband. Conrad Chisholm brushed aside questions of his "manhood" and helped in any way he could to further his wife's success in politics. For most women in Congress, the support and assistance of their husbands and family members is crucial. (Men in Congress, after all, need the complete support of their spouses and families, too.)

Chisholm won in her first bid for elected office. She went to Albany, New York's capital, with strong ideals and the courage to forge her own path. Because of her outspokenness, she was not a popular figure in the assembly. Soon, though, her colleagues realized she was a force to be reckoned with and one they could not stop.

Because the representatives in many state legislatures were away from home and their families, the atmosphere sometimes took on a festive tone. Male representatives found themselves with no familial responsibilities in the evenings, so they would dine together, socialize together, even go to bars together. They got to know one another on a personal level. But this social atmosphere proved to be a barrier that women are still trying to overcome. Women were not welcome in the chamber and they were not welcome at social gatherings. How, then, could female legislators develop professional relationships with their male colleagues? This question has plagued many women in politics and in business.

Chisholm solved this issue by making the other assembly members deal with her on her own terms. She made it very clear that she was in Albany to work, not to have a few laughs over cocktails. Eventually, her hard work, independence, and successful lobbying won her the respect of many of the assemblymen. She would use these same methods on Capitol Hill.

In 1968, redistricting presented Chisholm with the chance to run for Congress. Each congressional district is defined by geographic boundaries based in part on population statistics. Usually these boundaries are redrawn, or "redistricted," when the population changes—people moving in and out of the area over time. The task of redrawing a district falls to the state legislatures.

Legislators try to use redistricting in their favor, calculating how constituents will vote for their party's candidates. In Chisholm's case, the newly drawn district held many black and Latino voters. It was almost certain that an African-American would be elected from the Bedford-Stuyvesant area of Brooklyn, so Chisholm thought she had a good chance. But the Democratic powers felt differently. They wanted a black man for the job.

There were two things the Democrats hadn't counted on: first, Chisholm spoke Spanish, so she could communicate with Latino men and women in their own language; and second, more women than men were registered to vote in the district. Using this to her advantage, Chisholm rode around the district in a car marked with the slogan "Unbought and Unbossed." She talked with women leaving grocery stores and on PTA committees. Many were already familiar with her because of her work with New York's educational system. Others wanted to see a woman go to Washington to speak for them.

After a grueling and sometimes mean-spirited campaign, Chisholm won. She went to Congress as the first African-American woman representative and the only new woman elected to the House of Repre-

Shirley Chisholm in 1969 proposes a bill to require national minimum Federal standards of welfare. To her left is Edward I. Koch, then a new congressman who later became mayor of New York City.

sentatives in 1968. It wasn't long before the "trouble-maker" moniker was pinned on her again.

In addition to her maiden speech against the Vietnam War, Chisholm waged a very public campaign to get a committee assignment she felt she deserved. At first she was told to join the Forestry and Rural Development subcommittees of the House Agriculture Committee. Realizing that these issues had little to do with her poor urban constituents back home, she went right to the top and pleaded her case to Speaker of the House John McCormick. Predictably, he told her to wait her turn and do as she was told. What he didn't know was that Representative Chisholm would take those words as a direct challenge.

After some more protests, she defied the parliamentary ploys of her fellow congressmen and marched right down the aisle to the microphone in front of the Speaker's podium. She proceeded to introduce legislation to have herself reassigned, and a few weeks later Shirley Chisholm reported to the Veterans Committee. It wasn't her first choice, but as she said, "There are a lot more veterans in my district than trees!"

An active legislator and hard worker who eschewed the Washington social scene, Chisholm was nevertheless a media star and in great demand for speaking to college students around the country. Her status as the only African-American woman in Congress made her a beacon—blacks and women in America were looking to Shirley Chisholm to better their lives. She tried to fulfill this expectation as well as she could.

Chisholm is remembered by many for her presidential run. She never harbored any dreams of winning but insisted on the fight to improve the visibility of women in politics and in the Democratic Party. From the beginning, her campaign was plagued by poor management and no money. After running in a few presidential primaries, Chisholm wanted to make her point at the Democratic Convention and at least get on the first ballot. She went to her fellow black delegates to ask for their support. But they disappointed her with petty infighting and their own sexism. In 1972, the Democrats nominated George McGovern.

Although disappointed, Chisholm returned to Congress where she stayed until 1980, when she retired from elective politics to teach. But during her tenure she was instrumental in the development of the Congresswomen's Caucus, the National Political Women's Caucus, and the National Political Congress of Black Women, and in the fight for equal rights, gay and lesbian rights, and safe and legal abortions.

Chisholm is also known for her continued attempts to improve educational opportunities for African-Americans and women. In her maiden speech she called for Congress to rearrange its priorities, saying, "I am deeply disappointed at the clear evidence that the number-one priority of the new administration is to buy more and more and more weapons of war. . . . We must force the administration to rethink its distorted, unreal scale of priorities. Our children, our jobless men, our deprived, rejected, and starving fellow citizens must come first."[3]

On another explosive issue, abortion, Chisholm was outspoken. Abortion was an illegal procedure in 1968. But Representative Chisholm was familiar with the horror stories of poor women in her district seeking unsafe abortions out of desperation. After being asked to lead a new group called the National Association for the Repeal of Abortion Laws (NARAL) and receiving a huge amount of mail, Chisholm drafted legislation to repeal the restrictive abortion laws. She found no support among members of Congress who, even if they personally supported it, would not speak for it in public for fear of raising some difficult questions.

Representative Chisholm shifted her tactics and began to focus on grassroots programs and human services legislation that would make life better for women, minorities, and the poor. Chief among these were improving educational and employment opportunities. She championed bills in support of increasing the minimum wage, pushing for training programs, and protecting domestic workers, most of whom were women and minorities. (Chisholm's own mother worked as a cleaning woman for white families.)

It's interesting to note that Representative Chisholm was always walking a fine line between her work for women's rights and civil rights. In the women's movement she was the subject of racism and in the civil rights movement she was the subject of sexism. But there can be no doubt that "The Fighting Shirley Chisholm" left an indelible mark in both movements.

Congresswomen and the Vietnam War

Most women in Congress during the Vietnam War opposed it, as Mink and Chisholm did, but some felt otherwise. Representatives Louise Day Hicks (D–Mass.; rep. 1971–73) and Charlotte T. Reid (R–Ill.; rep. 1963–71) often supported military measures. Reid was the first member of Congress to be cleared to visit Vietnam. She spent four days flying over the jungle and talking with soldiers. The Vietnam War affected how women politicians acted and were treated, but in different and sometimes conflicting ways.

At a time when women were really just beginning to make headway into the world of politics, the perception of a woman against the war could be powerful. For some voters it meant that a woman wasn't "tough enough" to play in the real world. This argument was later used against Representative Geraldine Ferraro during her 1984 bid for the vice presidency.

And those who wielded it were successful at changing the discussion from real issues to talk of whether or not Representative Ferraro was "man enough." But for others, opposing war—the Vietnam War in particular—was a well-supported position.

It must be understood that the Vietnam War divided the country, the Congress, and even individual families. Tempers flared on the subject of American participation in what was widely considered to be a civil war far away in Asia. During the last half of the 1960s and throughout the 1970s, the antiwar movement grew to a cacophony of voices. Yet many of the protesters were associated with the fringes of society or the "anti-establishment." The label "hippie" was attached to the protesters in an attempt to dismiss their views.

To the majority of members of Congress, who were called the "establishment," vocal opposition to the war, marches, and peaceful and not-so-peaceful protests were an affront to the power and authority vested in Congress. For women members to join the protesters in speaking out against the war, even in a respectful manner, required courage and the knowledge that enemies would be made on both sides of the aisle. Worse, some women feared being associated with the "fringes" of society. This might weaken their political base, especially within their own parties.

Bella Abzug

Into the fray of the Vietnam War debate jumped Bella Savitzky Abzug (D–N.Y.; rep. 1971–76). Abzug honed much of her political skills working in the peace movement. She was unwilling to let perceptions and misguided public opinion polls distract her from what she knew was right.

Like her or despise her (and many people did), Bella Abzug made a definite dent during her six years in Congress. Although many like to point to her loud mouth, brashness, and aggressive tactics, Representative Abzug should be credited with strengthening the foundation of the women's movement and the position of women in Congress.

Abzug understood power plays and the strategies involved in the game of politics. Her whole life has been a balancing act between using this knowledge to stay in politics and fighting for individual justice. Her outspokenness and use of "politics" made her few friends in Congress. But she grew into a hero for many women and for disenfranchised groups of minorities and the poor.

Bella Savitzky was born in 1920 to immigrant Jewish parents who instilled in her a passion for human rights. Even at a very young age Bella was pounding the pavement, collecting money to help build a Jewish homeland in Israel. She was still young when she decided to become a lawyer. After receiving a reply from Harvard that it did not accept women, Bella went to Columbia Law School, just a subway stop away from where she lived with her mother. (Her father died when she was thirteen).

Fighting for social justice is what drives Abzug. It's why she became a lawyer, it's why she fought so vehemently to stop the war in Vietnam, it's why she became a candidate for Congress, and it's why she remains such an active player in global politics. Her 1970 campaign slogan, "This woman's place is in the house—the House of Representatives," was transformed into a feminist rallying cry, "A woman's place is in the House—and the Senate!"

Abzug said, "I'm going to Congress because I think Congress needs women. There's no diversity there, I'm going to fight for women's rights."[4] In fact, Abzug

ERA
ERA YES
ERA NWPC
ERA

felt very strongly that fighting for women's rights was akin to social justice. She believes that different groups must band together in their fight for equality. "It isn't enough for individual groups to organize only around their own needs. They must also coalesce with others who share the same ideas and have similar needs. Women's issues are not separate from the interest of everyone in this country. You cannot eliminate sexism unless you also eliminate racism, poverty and institutional violence at home and abroad—all go together. The woman's movement is therefore a humanist movement."[5] Such coalition-building echoes the politics of the early 1900s, when women fought hard for their own rights but at the same time sought help for others who were disenfranchised.

Like Shirley Chisholm, Abzug helped many men get elected to office over the years. When one of them, frustrated with her demands and pressure, finally told her to run for office herself, she did. She realized that all the men she helped elect "weren't any more qualified or able than I, and in some cases they were less so."[6]

After arriving in Congress in 1971, one of the first things she did was join with Representative Chisholm to hold hearings on the child-care needs of working women. Later they introduced legislation to respond to these needs.

The men in Congress used every chance they could to demean Representative Abzug. If they put a focus on her looks and appearance then they could

Bella Abzug (left) and feminist leader Betty Friedan wear ERA (Equal Rights Amendment) sashes and buttons at the Democratic National Convention in New York in 1980.

detract from the power of her ideas. They had considered women in Congress to be ladies; they expected women on Capitol Hill to act accordingly, to be nice and gracious, and not speak too loudly. It meant tending to women's business that did not interest the men, and looking like a "lady."

Representative Abzug decidedly did not fit any of these descriptions. In one famous exchange, Vice President Spiro Agnew spoke at a Republican fundraiser and exclaimed that the Republicans must do whatever they can to "keep Bella Abzug from showing up in Congress in hot pants." Representative Abzug's response was, "Hot pants will disappear from the national scene, along with Mr. Agnew and Mr. Nixon." Her prediction was correct, as both Agnew and Nixon left Washington in disgrace. (Hot pants went out of style, too!)

It was a humorous exchange, but what's important to notice is that it was fair game for a man to complain or joke about a congresswoman's appearance. Even if Vice President Agnew had made a similar joke about a congressman in polka dots or a bad suit, the jab wouldn't have had the same sexual insinuation. Subtle sex discrimination is a powerful force. In this instance, it meant that Agnew could control the debate: he could discuss how Representative Abzug looked and thereby ignore what she thought. As a woman, her opinions and ideas about the issues were second to her appearance and to how well she fit the mold of "lady."

Bella Abzug would have none of it. In fact, early in her law career she took to wearing big, colorful hats. She did this, she said, because so many other lawyers and judges were assuming she was a secretary instead of an attorney. Abzug's hats continued to be her trademark. In her 1972 autobiography, *I, a Woman,* she wrote, "There are those who say I'm impatient, impetuous, uppity, rude, profane, brash, and overbearing. Whether I'm any of these things, or all of them, you can decide for yourself. But whatever I am—and this ought to be made very clear at the outset—I am a very serious woman."[7]

Away from the publicity, Representative Abzug was involved in several major pieces of legislation. She worked with Representative Mink to pass the Title IX amendment; helped to extend the Equal Pay Act of 1963 to cover administrative, professional, and executive employees; introduced abortion rights legislation; and worked for the Equal Rights Amendment. Back in her home district in New York, Abzug saved housing from being destroyed, worked to limit rent increases, obtained funds for police protection for elderly people living in high-crime areas, and organized other programs to help the poverty-stricken.

Much of Representative Abzug's time was spent building a national network of women working to get other women elected. She was one of the founders of the National Women's Political Caucus along with Betty Friedan, Gloria Steinem, Representative Chisholm, and civil rights activist Myrlie Evers. Within Washington she pushed for the formation of a Congresswomen's Caucus but met with little success. It wasn't until after Abzug left Congress that another New York Democrat, Representative Elizabeth Holtzman, took the reins and was finally able to establish a women's caucus on Capitol Hill.

Today, Bella Abzug enjoys an elder stateswoman status and remains extremely involved in women's rights from a global perspective. She attended the 1995 United Nations Conference on Women held in Beijing, China, and led the delegation from her organization, Women's Environment and Development Organization (WEDO).

As for her detractors, who used to complain about

her combative manner, she says, "I am very much the same person I was when I entered Congress, but more people have come to agree with me. Therefore they consider my touch is softer."[8]

Barbara Jordan

In the annals of political history there will rarely be remembered a representative more compelling, articulate, or dignified than Barbara Jordan (D–Tex.; rep. 1973–79). With a tall frame and a voice like God, Barbara Jordan was one of the most respected members of Congress by men and women, white and black, Republican and Democrat.

Before her election to Congress in 1972, she was already well known, not only for her intellect and legislative career but for being the first woman elected to the Texas State Senate in 1966 and the first African-American elected to that chamber since 1882. When she went on to the U.S. House—as the first African-American from the South elected to Congress since the Reconstruction era—she quickly made her mark during the Watergate hearings, one of the most infamous periods in American history.

Born to a poor African-American couple in Houston, Texas, Barbara Jordan aspired to help others and become a full participant in the political process. After completing high school in Houston's segregated public schools, she went to the all-black Texas Southern University, where she was head of the debating team. She recalled the great sense of achievement when her debating team tied in a match with Harvard University. She said, "When an all-black team ties Harvard, it wins."[9]

Her next step was to go to law school, and she applied to Harvard University. She was turned down, so she earned her law degree across the Charles River at

Boston University. She returned to Texas and set up a small law practice out of her home. After directing a voting drive to support the presidential team of John Kennedy and Lyndon Johnson, Jordan decided to run for office herself. It took her three tries, but she won a seat in the Texas state senate. This began her political career in a state known for the corruption and childish "boys will be boys" antics of its legislature. Jordan's friend, political commentator Molly Ivins, covered the Texas legislature as a reporter and columnist. She once wrote, "Texas politicians aren't crooks; it's just that they tend to have an overdeveloped sense of the extenuatin' circumstance. As they say around the Legislature, if you can't drink their whisky . . . take their money, and vote against 'em anyway, you don't belong in office."[10]

Undaunted, Barbara Jordan strode into the Texas legislature with an air of confidence. When she finally walked out of that chamber on her way to Washington in January 1973, she received a standing ovation from all her Texan colleagues.

Imagine what it must have been like for Jordan to enter into a conservative, white male state-house. Jordan's detractors didn't think she (or any other black woman) had a chance of making any kind of significant contribution in that environment. But contribute she did. After studying the style of the legislature's leaders, Representative Jordan learned the importance of parliamentary procedures (the rules of order that govern a meeting and the passing of laws). Step by step she earned the respect of her colleagues.

Jordan's skill in passing bills grew, and after her first year she was voted the outstanding freshman legislator. Then she became the president *pro tempore*, which meant that she was next in line to lead the state after the governor and the lieutenant governor. In Texas there is a tradition by which the governor and the lieutenant governor both leave the state on the same day to give the senate president *pro tempore* the opportunity to be sworn in as "Governor for a day." Although it was only symbolic, Barbara Jordan became the first and only black woman to be sworn in as governor of any state.

Although it took her three tries to get elected to the state legislature, she needed only one try to win a seat in the U.S. House. And she won big, with more than 80 percent of the vote. Her district was largely a poor one made up of poverty-stricken blacks and whites. With that many votes in her favor, Jordan understood that "lots of white people voted for me too." She took this message seriously and did her best to represent all of her constituents.

Upon arriving in Washington, the first measure of business for the new congresswoman was to strengthen the Voting Rights Act. This legislation was supposed to assure every American, black and white, rich and poor, the means to vote in elections. But before it could take up much of Jordan's time, the scandal that gripped the nation took center stage.

The story of Watergate is inextricably woven with that of Jordan, who sat on the House Judiciary Committee for her term beginning in January 1973. Republican Richard M. Nixon had just been reelected president. But scandal broke early in the year when it was revealed that someone had broken into the Democratic Party Headquarters based in the Watergate Hotel apartment complex in Washington, D.C. Soon word began leaking out that the president himself was implicated in this impropriety. But the crux of Watergate, and Nixon's final downfall, was a series of recordings made in the Oval Office. Although ordered to hand them over, Nixon refused. The tapes would have made it clear that he was a driving force behind the Watergate break-in.

Barbara Jordan delivering opening remarks before the House Judiciary Committee's debate of the impeachment of President Richard Nixon in July 1974

What did Barbara Jordan have to do with all this? Plenty. As a member of the House Judiciary Committee, she listened to months and months of testimony. The committee was essentially deciding whether or not to bring impeachment proceedings against the president. It would have been only the second time in U.S. history that a sitting president was impeached, or forced to leave office. (The first was Andrew Johnson, in 1868.)

In a televised speech, freshman Congresswoman Barbara Jordan spoke of the Constitution and reminded the Congress and the American public exactly what impeachment meant. Her methodical history lesson was an example of perfect pitch. She combined her personal feelings of the situation with her personal admiration and respect for the Constitution. She set this against the backdrop of a president who had abused his powers, and worse, had "subverted the Constitution." Millions of Americans were watching the hearings on television, and Barbara Jordan was an instant celebrity:

> *"We, the people" it is a very eloquent beginning. But when the Constitution of the United States was completed on the 17th of September in 1787, I was not included in that "We, the people." I felt for many years that somehow George Washington and Alexander Hamilton just left me out by mistake. But through the process of amendment, interpretation, and court decision, I have finally been included in "We, the people."*

With these eloquent words, Representative Jordan reminded the world what the Constitution truly means and why it was so important not to let Richard Nixon abuse its powers. Her speech continued to explain in great detail what it meant to impeach a president and why it applied to Richard Nixon. The committee voted in favor of proceeding with the impeachment, and it was soon to be up to the full House for a vote. But President Nixon spared the country this humiliation and resigned on August 8, 1974, effective at noon the next day.

Barbara Jordan made history again in 1976 when she was a keynote speaker at the Democratic National Convention in New York City—the first woman and the first African-American to have that honor. The other speaker was a representative from Ohio, former astronaut John Glenn. When Representative Jordan took the stage at Madison Square Garden, a thunderous applause filled the arena. She began:

> *One hundred and forty-four years ago, members of the Democratic Party first met in convention to select a presidential candidate. Since that time Democrats have continued to convene once every four years and draft a party platform and nominate a presidential candidate. And our meeting this week is a continuation of that tradition.*
>
> *But there is something different about tonight. There is something special about tonight. What is different? What is special? I, Barbara Jordan, am a keynote speaker.*

In these brief remarks, Representative Jordan had summed up the progress made by African-Americans and by women as represented by her role in that convention. Just four years earlier, Representative Shirley Chisholm was arguing with her fellow black delegates about her bid to get on the first ballot for the Democratic nomination for president!

Representative Jordan was reelected twice and served in Congress from 1973 to 1979. She was disappointed with the leaders of the Democratic Party and their unwillingness to move her into a leadership position. Feeling she could accomplish more of her goals in other ways, she returned to Texas to teach political ethics at the University of Texas Lyndon B. Johnson School of Public Affairs. She embedded in her students her faith in the Constitution (she always carried a copy with her) and her resolute belief that public officials must be held accountable. She said, "We must provide the people with a vision of the future."

Barbara Jordan suffered from multiple sclerosis but was no less formidable in her wheelchair. She enjoyed an active schedule of public speaking and writing. She also continued to speak out on political issues and remained active in politics. In 1995 she was the chairwoman of the Commission on Immigration Reform and spoke out against denying citizenship to the children of illegal immigrants. She died in January 1996 of complications from leukemia. Jordan was fifty-nine years old.

Patricia Schroeder

After more than twenty years of service in the House of Representatives, Pat Schroeder (D–Colo.; rep. 1973–97) became the top-ranking woman in the House and was considered the Dean of Congresswomen. She is one of only four women ever to have chaired a House committee. She is at the forefront of debate on family issues, military issues, and other civil rights issues. She was even a potential candidate for president.

With this type of résumé one would expect Representative Schroeder to be a major leader in the Democratic Party. Unfortunately, this has not been the case, even though she served as a Democratic whip since 1978 and was appointed a deputy whip in 1987. If the Democrats had retained the majority of House seats in 1994, Representative Schroeder would have become the chair of the Post Office and Civil Service Committee. Instead, the Republicans won the majority and Schroeder's chance at a committee chair vanished. (In fact, the entire Post Office and Civil Service Committee was abolished.) When Americans think of the Democratic Party or Congress, they do not automatically think of Pat Schroeder as a leader. Perhaps this is because she has always tried to reframe the debate to include talk of the needs of women and minorities.

Pat Schroeder is the first to tell you she has a wicked sense of humor and a wit to match even the harshest attack—she is not always one to act like a "lady." While campaigning for her first election in 1972, Schroeder was asked again and again how she could run for office when she had two children to raise and a husband to take care of. Schroeder jokingly replied that she and her husband simply put the children into the freezer each morning, go to work, and return home to defrost the family. Not everyone thought it was funny.

Then again, not everyone who has just won a seat in the U.S. House of Representatives is shown in the newspapers the next day telling her children it's time to go to bed. Male winners were shown giving a speech or simply smiling into the camera. But that's not how women victors were treated by the press twenty-five years ago. It took the media many more years to focus on Representative Schroeder's ideas and opinions.

Born in Portland, Oregon, Pat Nell Scott moved around the country with her family. She stopped at the University of Minnesota, where she graduated *magna cum laude* ("with high honors") in 1961. She attended Harvard Law School—classmates included Representative Elizabeth Holtzman and U.S. Attorney General Janet Reno—and moved to Denver, where she practiced law and taught. She married James Schroeder and raised two children. After all that, she won election to the U.S. House.

Representative Schroeder was a tireless crusader for women's equality, known for her battle to have women's health issues and research undertaken by the National Institutes of Health. As a senior member of the Armed Services Committee (one of very few women to gain power in this male bastion) she went to bat for all the women and men in the military.

Schroeder made her reputation on issues of children and family. Like Representatives Chisholm and Abzug, she is interested in helping better the everyday lives of women and men. But to do this, she works to overcome the discrimination that lingers in so many areas of life.

As chair of the House Select Committee on Children, Youth, and Families (this committee was abolished by the GOP at the start of the 104th Congress in 1995), Representative Schroeder wrote the Family and Medical Leave Act, which was signed into law by President Bill Clinton in 1993. She also wrote a book, *Champion of the Great American Family*, on the subject of families and the issues they face. As a member of the Armed Services Committee, Schroeder has fought against a growing Defense Department. She exposed and opposed the waste and fraud that has come to be associated with defense spending. But at the same time she fights for better pay and opportunities for people in the military. She wrote and passed the Military Family Act of 1985, which improved the benefits of military families.

Like Shirley Chisholm, Pat Schroeder had dreams of running for the White House. But in 1988 in a publicized event during which she shed some tears, she announced her decision not to run. The press and others seized on this display of emotion to prove that women were not "tough enough" to be in politics. Schroeder retorted, "I stand accused . . . of failure to be a role model [for women politicians]. What is the role? Joan of Arc? Annie Oakley? The female equivalent of Dirty Harry?" Indeed, Pat Schroeder chose not to conform to the stereotype of the politician—the male politician. Instead she showed she was human

Pat Schroeder in 1985 arguing for changes in the methods of protecting U.S. national security secrets

and felt deeply about the direction the country was headed. She contends that "the American people are more ready for a woman in the White House than Washington is."

She is known for her support of liberal issues and women's issues. She works for abortion rights, equal rights for women, civil rights for lesbians and gay men, and help for other social groups denied their full rights. She was also a driving force behind the formation of the Congressional Caucus for Women's Issues and served as its co-chair.

Schroeder's sharp tongue alternately won her accolades and scorn. When she packaged a strong sound bite attacking the opposition, her fellow Democrats applauded. But when she complained about the lack of will in Congress to "face reality" and attack tough problems, her colleagues were not pleased.

To millions of Americans—men and women alike—Pat Schroeder was the conscience of Congress. She could be counted on to address the difficult and unpopular subjects other politicians are scared to broach. Representative Schroeder confirmed herself as a role model during the Clarence Thomas Supreme Court confirmation hearings in 1991. She didn't know it at the time, but her leadership in this situation helped start a revolution in America. Whether they believed Anita Hill or Clarence Thomas, men and women alike began to understand the pervasiveness of sexual harassment in the workplace. Educational programs were developed, there was an increase in the number of complaints filed with authorities, and general awareness was raised on the issue. The whole face of Congress changed, too, as the number of congresswomen rose to forty-seven after the 1992 elections. This was by far the largest percentage of women to be seated in any one session of Congress.

Although the number of women in Congress remained constant after the 1994 elections, the tone of Capitol Hill changed. When Schroeder announced her resignation, effective January 1997, many thought it was because Congress had become so combative. But Schroeder said:

> *The current kill-or-be-killed political climate is not why I'm retiring. That doesn't cause me to run and hide, although I don't like the tenor of politics in the current Congress. The tone is nastier now than ever before. . . . I hope that by getting out of Congress and having something of an emeritus status, people will listen to me a little more, instead of just dismissing me as another politician.*[11]

6

Getting Together: The Congressional Caucus on Women's Issues

THERE IS MUCH activity in Congress and many players. Those who participate in activities and committees outside the chamber usually have an easier time getting access to the congressmen who can help make or break a deal. After all, power and the access to power are two major factors in getting things accomplished in politics. One way to gain this access is to sit on an influential committee like Appropriations, preferably to chair it. But women were rarely considered for these top jobs. By the 1972 elections it was clear that women were in Congress to stay. Their numbers were growing, but they were still meeting with great disappointment when committee leadership positions were doled out.

There is power in numbers, and members of Congress look for common ground among themselves to

Audrey Rowe (second from left) of the National Women's Political Caucus joins congresswomen Millicent Fenwick, Margaret Heckler, and Bella Abzug in 1975.

form unions, or voting blocks. Sometimes this is as simple as joining one's political party caucus. Sometimes the similarities, such as race or gender, transcend party lines. These groups sometimes band together to form a "caucus." Caucuses are sanctioned by Congress and may receive official recognition, meeting rooms for gatherings, even some financial support. Over the years there have been caucuses for African-Americans, blue-collar workers, even sportsmen.

Caucuses are important to the inner workings of Congress. During their meetings members discuss the issues they consider especially important. They work together, often across party lines, to pass certain legislation or at least to educate their fellow members in the House or Senate.

Building a Women's Caucus

In the early 1970s eleven to nineteen women were members of Congress at any one time. From an outsider's perspective it would make sense that these women work together, both to pass legislation of importance to women across the country and to fight for respect among their male colleagues. But an outsider's perspective on Washington can miss some important subtleties, especially when it comes to making sense of Congress.

Two qualities can help a member rise to positions of power: seniority and a "go along to get along" approach. Because most of the women in Congress were relative newcomers, they held little power in terms of getting influential committee assignments. It was also difficult to build coalitions on the floor because they did not have the seniority to be recognized. The cycle of power kept this potent mixture in the hands of a very few people. In Congress, before freshman or newer members will be successful in a new venture, they must have the blessing of more senior members, especially those who represent the leadership of their political party. And to get this needed support, they must have a few senior members who are willing to speak up and get involved.

In 1975 many of the younger female members were eager to gather together. Among the most outspoken were Bella Abzug, Shirley Chisholm, and Barbara Mikulski. But as Representative Abzug set out to create a women's caucus in her usual abrasive fashion, she was met with great resistance. Abzug rarely "went along to get along." As a result, even if she had a good idea, others were wary of siding with her for fear of what she might say or do next.

A more senior member, Leonor Sullivan (D–Mo.; rep. 1953–77), felt that Abzug was too unpredictable. She let it be known that she felt a women's caucus was a bad idea. She was not the only senior female member to resist the notion. Representative Sullivan had been in Congress for several terms and had worked her way up the committee ladder one rung at a time. She rarely made waves and had gradually earned the begrudging respect of her male colleagues.

Representative Sullivan also held some very traditional views on the roles of women. She was adamant that a woman not seek office until after she had fulfilled her duties as wife and mother. Sullivan was the only woman in the House to vote against the Equal Rights Amendment, and she insisted people refer to her as "Mrs. John Sullivan." She even tried to establish a dress code so that women could not wear slacks in the House chamber. Imagine these two politicians trying to negotiate the formation of a women's caucus!

The differences between Sullivan and Abzug demonstrate why the beginnings of the Congresswomen's Caucus were so rife with disagreement and dead ends. Long-serving congresswomen such as Sullivan, Edith Green (D–Oregon; rep. 1955–75), and Julia Butler Hansen (D–Wash.; rep. 1960–75), were concerned that a women's caucus would be viewed by their male colleagues as the women "ganging up" on the men. They worried about the value of such an organization, and even its legitimacy. All three of these women had been reelected term after term and had earned the respect of their male colleagues the old-fashioned way—they had put in their time and remained acutely aware of the formalities and rules of the House. If they brought attention to themselves as women, the tactic might backfire, thus bringing on the wrath of the men and the concern of their constituents.

Junior congresswomen such as Representatives Abzug, Chisholm, Schroeder, and Mikulski felt otherwise. They were ready to eschew some of the old guard's archaic unwritten laws in favor of making sure their voices were heard, even at the risk of offending some of their colleagues. But it wasn't until Bella Abzug left the House that they began to make progress. Another New York Democrat, Elizabeth Holtzman, joined with Massachusetts Republican Margaret M. Heckler (R–Mass.; rep. 1967–82) to form what is now called the Congressional Caucus on Women's Issues (originally call the Congresswomen's Caucus).

Making it Happen

Outside Washington, D.C., the feminist movement was in full gear in the late 1970s. Activists and organizers such as Gloria Steinem, Betty Friedan, Bella Abzug, and Shirley Chisholm helped create two very important national organizations: the National Organization for Women (NOW) and the National Women's Political Caucus (NWPC). Both are still in existence, still lobbying Congress and educating the public on issues of concern to American women. The NWPC was created to help gain access to "the powers that be" in Washington. Their goal is to bring women together to draft their ideas and responses to issues, then present them to members of Congress. The hope is that their concerns will not only be heard but will be taken seriously.

Although the women's movement was progressing outside the nation's Capitol, change in women's status within Congress was slow, strained, and strategized. Congresswomen had to consider their own needs along with those of their constituents. They had to be sensitive to the leadership of Congress and the leadership of their political parties. All of these people mattered (not to mention their own families and friends and personal lives). With so many people to please, it's no wonder that the formation of a caucus dedicated to women took so long to come to fruition.

If all of these pressures weren't enough, Holtzman, Heckler, Chisholm, and others had to overcome the obstacles presented by their sister representatives who believed that women should adhere to traditional roles. Also, the word "feminist" was considered a sign of hostility. (Indeed, for many people, it still is.) Even friendly voices didn't understand. Representatives Hansen and Green did not see much benefit in a women's caucus, even though they believed in equal rights and agreed that sex discrimination in Congress was rampant.

In 1977 things began to change when representatives Holtzman, a Democrat, and Heckler, a Republican, reached across the aisle. Together they took meaningful steps to create an organization that would stand the test of time and serve an important purpose. Holtzman was determined to make it succeed, and she put much energy into the administrative tasks. Meanwhile, Heckler used her skills as a coalition builder to gain support from other representatives and from the congressional leadership.

With the help of representatives Chisholm and Mikulski, the first meeting of the Congresswomen's

Caucus was held on April 19, 1977. Only four congresswomen attended the meeting (though there were eighteen women in Congress at the time). After a few meetings, the scheduled time and location were adjusted to better accommodate schedules. Within a few months, more members were attending meetings on a regular basis. In a few years, the Congresswomen's Caucus was taken seriously by members of Congress and all those involved in politics.

In addition to meetings where issues and Caucus business were discussed, guest speakers were on the agenda. These included members of the president's cabinet and top-level administrators of congressional departments. The meetings were an exchange where Caucus members educated their speakers on issues that concerned them and the speakers in turn educated Caucus members on their respective specialties.

Growing Pains

As the Caucus found steady ground on which to operate, it also experienced the growing pains that often afflict young organizations. Financial support was uncertain, and without money, there was little the Caucus could accomplish. The activities of the Caucus were above and beyond the already demanding schedules and budgets of the congresswomen. They had precious little time and few staff members to spare.

The Caucus was originally put together to discuss improving the selection of committee assignments for congresswomen. Committee assignments, of course, represent power in Congress, and the women felt that they were not granted the same access as their male colleagues. But Caucus members soon realized that they could achieve more than just power plays like committee assignments.

When Abzug and Holtzman envisioned the Caucus, they had in mind an array of activities. They saw women of all political persuasions united in a chorus of education and influence to further the status of women in America. The reality was that each Caucus member had different opinions about most issues. Abortion, for instance, was one touchy subject that they all agreed not to discuss.

So if they held different beliefs, how could they work together? Since it was clear that Caucus members would not agree on everything, it was decided that they would take on only those issues they all agreed upon. Whenever a vote was taken among them or a letter passed around for signatures, every Caucus member had to climb on board or the initiative would go no further. Needless to say, this rule may have made it easier to interest women from both parties in joining the Caucus, but it also proved to restrict the Caucus from fomenting any real change. The administrative and ideological problems were blatant. Getting everyone's agreement on language and subject matter proved a very laborious task for a fledgling new group. And it was a problem that would be addressed several times over the next twenty years.

Other problems facing the Caucus included difficulty gaining recognition from some presidential administrations, financial instability, limited staff, the lack of interest among many congresswomen, and pressure from the media. The Caucus co-chairs (there is always a chair from each party) were continually asked why every female member of Congress wasn't in the Caucus. (Imagine the challenge of having to explain why a woman wouldn't join a women's caucus.) The reasons several congresswomen never joined, or joined in name only, are steeped in party politics and image. The Caucus had liberal leanings, and some Republican members were nervous about associating with such a liberal group. In the 1980s President Ronald Reagan tried to disband the Caucus by making its operating rules more restrictive. Several of the new Republican members didn't want to risk angering the president, even if they agreed with much of the Caucus's platform.

With so many challenges, why did these women fight so hard and so long to establish this organization? Because the rewards are great. As a group, these women were able to share knowledge and get much-needed support for issues of great importance to them. Instead of having to be experts on all issues, Caucus members shared the burden. Often one member would be the expert on a few matters and educate her peers when necessary. This meant that members could have an effect on a great deal of legislation while having to master only a few issues. The workload was shared.

Although Caucus members didn't agree on every subject, members knew that their voices and opinions were important. They could get a "reality check" when sexism in their political or daily lives became too commonplace. The Caucus helped congresswomen name the inequalities facing them and their female constituents. Inequalities ranged from not having a women's bathroom for female senators to sexual harassment and violence against women.

The Caucus also provided an avenue to the business sector and to the women's movement. Members like Representative Chisholm, who were very active on the lecture circuit, could share information and help promote a national dialogue. Also, the Congresswomen's Caucus on occasion developed alliances with other congressional caucuses such as the Black Caucus or the Democratic Study Group.

The Caucus Today

The Caucus has had many illustrious co-chairs over the years, such as Pat Schroeder, Olympia Snowe, and Geraldine Ferraro. Yet even these talented women could not protect the Caucus from great change. In

1982, new Reagan-inspired financial regulations restricted the type of funding the Caucus could receive. Also, Caucus members began to realize that they could benefit from the support of their male colleagues. This discussion had been held many times before. One argument held that many men were very supportive of women's issues and could lend much to the Caucus. The other side argued that men might dilute the focus of the Caucus.

This debate was settled in 1982 when the Caucus changed its name to the "Congressional Caucus for Women's Issues" and opened the membership to any member of Congress, female or male. Soon more than a hundred men had joined! By 1990 the Caucus enjoyed a membership of 150 men and women.

Over the years the Caucus has been involved in many activities, from helping to pass the Equal Rights Amendment to legislation helping low-income women. Because of the intense budget cuts forced on the Caucus in the 1980s, congresswomen now rely on outside women's organizations to do some of the research and lobbying that might have been handled by the Caucus. Nevertheless, the Caucus was still taking the lead in family issues and gender equity issues. Although women's issues are not always at the forefront of Congress's agenda, they have become part of the fabric of American politics. Sexual harassment, working mothers, violence against women, equal pay—these issues are dealt with on a daily basis, with support from men and women, politicians, and activists. In an interview about the Caucus in September 1994, Co-Chair Olympia Snowe said, "We have some vast differences philosophically, but it is amazing how we come together on issues of importance to women."[1]

The Caucus continues to hold regular bi-partisan strategy sessions, they still meet for women-only dinners, and they carry on the struggle for fairness and equality in American life and politics.

2

Geraldine Ferraro

RUNNING FOR THE vice presidency of the United States was Geraldine Ferraro's crowning moment and her greatest downfall. Although she was not the first woman to have tried for this office, Ferraro was the first to rise through the ranks of a major political party that backed her run for the nation's number-two spot. She was the first woman candidate for this office to be taken seriously by her peers, the press, and the voters.

Her running mate, Walter Mondale, was fully cognizant of the historic step he was taking when he decided to choose a woman partner. The year was 1984, and the Reagan-Bush team was unstoppable. Reagan's Republican administration had been leading the country for four years and was still extremely popular. Even so, the Democrats wanted to put up a solid

Geraldine Ferraro in 1984

fight for the White House. The realization that winning would be a long shot was perhaps a vote in favor of taking more risks than usual with the campaign. Mondale considered his choices carefully and even interviewed several other women (including Dianne Feinstein, then mayor of San Francisco) before settling on Ferraro.

Geraldine Ferraro embodied the American dream. The daughter of Italian immigrants in New York state, Ferraro was a young girl when her father died. Her mother, determined to care for her two children on her own, went to work as a seamstress. She managed to earn enough money to send Gerry to private school and then to college.

After settling on a career as a teacher (she was dissuaded from following her dream of medical school), Ferraro became bored. She decided to attend law school at night and completed her law degree. She married John Zaccaro in 1960 and they had three children. The Ferraro-Zaccaro family was close-knit. John ran his father's real estate business and Geraldine worked there part-time. She decided to practice law full-time and got a job in the New York District Attorney's office. There she developed a reputation as an aggressive prosecutor and became the head of a new unit called the Special Victim's Bureau. This unit dealt mainly with horrible crimes, and Ferraro became an expert and advocate on subjects society rarely likes to discuss—domestic abuse and child abuse.

In 1977, Ferraro decided to run for office. At her husband's urging, she set her sights on the U.S. House of Representatives. At this point she had little backing from the Democratic Party. So she campaigned the old-fashioned way, getting the required signatures by standing on street corners, shaking hands and talking to people. Her campaign was a success, using the slogan "At last . . . a tough, independent Democrat." She went to Washington to join the other sixteen women in Congress at the time. Her husband went with her to Washington but soon returned home to Queens because his business demanded his attention. To keep her family together, Ferraro settled into a schedule of returning to New York every Thursday. She spent the weekend in her district with her husband and children and enjoyed Sunday-night dinners with her mother and mother-in-law.

Working in Washington

Of course the press immediately asked Representative Ferraro if she had come to Washington to speak for America's women. (When was the last time a male member of Congress was asked if he came to Washington to speak for America's men?) Her reply was that she was there to serve her constituents, especially the disadvantaged.

Representative Ferraro was a good soldier and went along to get along. She acquiesced to the Democratic Party leadership in the House when it was expedient and chose her battles when her conscience demanded. It wasn't long before she caught the eye of Speaker of the House Tip O'Neill. Speaker O'Neill became an important mentor for her and was instrumental in teaching her how to obtain the power needed to get things done in Congress. Representative Ferraro also allied herself with President Jimmy Carter.

These alliances served her well. And on the question of gender, Representative Ferraro was not under any illusions about her rise to power in the Democratic Party. She once said,

Would I have gotten to where I am in the Congress in a little over four years if I weren't a woman? . . . I'd like to think they recognized me as a genius but what happens is, the Speaker has twelve women and all these guys and invariably somebody will say "We need a Commission and don't forget the women," so they're reaching out to those twelve time and time again because that's all they've got. . . . Maybe five women might say "I want to move forward, I want to help the party, I want to get involved in this or that," so it becomes very obvious and you become very well known. Would this happen to a fellow? No, so there are advantages to being a woman in Congress, advantages and disadvantages.[1]

In return, Representative Ferraro was a hardworking member who was known for doing her homework before speaking on a subject. In her district, she fought the battles of the myriad ethnic groups who lived in Queens. It was not unusual for her to intervene on behalf of immigrant Jews, Turks, or others who needed a voice in Washington. Nor was it unusual for Ferraro to team up with the other women in the House when such teamwork would expedite a solution. For instance, she worked with Representatives Schroeder and Mary Rose Oakar (D.–Ohio; rep. 1977–93) when each chaired a subcommittee interested in equal pay issues. Together, they had their subcommittees hold hearings on pay comparability.

Representative Ferraro was continually reelected by her constituents, giving her a little more freedom to become interested in national and international issues. She went on fact-finding missions to trouble spots around the globe; became involved in pressing social issues helping poverty-stricken children and older people; and was a tireless champion of women's rights and the Equal Rights Amendment. She also

Geraldine Ferraro at the residence of Democratic presidential candidate Walter Mondale in June 1984, shortly before he chose her as his vice presidential running mate

served as co-chair of the Congressional Caucus on Women's issues.

Ferraro's Roman Catholic upbringing was very important to her. But when it came to one of our nation's most divisive issues, abortion, she had a hard time reconciling her beliefs. After searching deep inside herself, she found a platform that was comfortable for her, but not for the Catholic Church. She explained that as a Catholic she was personally against abortion. But she was a strong proponent of a woman's right to choose, and she fought in Congress to have federal funds available for abortions. This public stance cost her official support from her own church. In a much publicized war of words, the archbishop of New York publicly chastised her and was determined to smear her name. But Representative Ferraro did not back down, even in the face of condemnation from her religious leaders. She rebutted by saying she was in Congress to "defend the right to religious freedom."

A slow, steady ascent to power followed for Representative Ferraro. She was known to be loyal to the Democratic Party and became a member of the executive committee of the Democratic Caucus. But it wasn't until a group of female political insiders suggested she think about the vice presidency that Ferraro thought there was merit in the idea. For the upcoming Democratic Convention in 1984 she became the first woman to be appointed Platform Chair, an important position. The platform chair has a great deal of influence in determining the tone and business of the convention. This feat, thought Ferraro, was major enough. But her supporters thought there was much more work to be done.

A Damaging Scandal

In the beginning Geraldine Ferraro made an ideal candidate. She was articulate, had a wonderful sense of humor, appealed to many different interest groups, had an excellent record of service, and exuded an aura of warmth and confidence. Plus, she was known as a "tough Democrat," balancing the liberal image of the party with some moderate positions. But in its usual fashion, the press treated Ferraro with no mercy and soon began an inquiry that has since become standard fare for anyone attempting to hold elective office.

She agreed to release her tax returns and those of her husband. A campaign law required a certain amount of disclosure, and Ferraro was comfortable going one step further. Her finances were separate from her husband's, and the media expected that he would release the same information. This was unlike anything that had come before. No male candidate has been expected to have his wife release any financial information. Perhaps this is because the perception of the American family was that of a husband who worked and earned money and a wife who stayed home to raise children and run the household. But by the 1970s and 1980s this had changed. Married couples, often with both husband and wife as wage-earners, owned things together and separately. Still, no male candidate was ever judged according to any kind of wealth or prominence belonging to his wife.

For candidate Ferraro, it was assumed that her husband was the one for whom it was important to disclose financial information. Aware that she was a "first," Ferraro did her best to accommodate an often-hostile press corps. In a press conference where she discussed some sketchy findings of back taxes and a business deal of her husband's gone bad, Ferraro kept her composure. Even her sense of humor remained after every last question had been answered.

Needless to say, this debacle clouded all the other election-year issues and took on a life of its own. Scandal has a way of overshadowing important concerns to ensure hot headlines. But Ferraro kept focused. She had an excellent debate with GOP vice presidential candidate George Bush (who went on to become president in 1988). One of the moderators, news anchor Dan Rather, felt he had to ask:

Congresswoman Ferraro, you have had little or no experience in military matters and yet you might someday find yourself commander in chief of the armed forces. How can you convince the American people and the potential enemy that you would know what to do to protect this nation's security, and do you think in any way the Soviets might be tempted to try to take advantage of you simply because you are a woman?

Here she was on national television defending her ability to lead the country into war. Ferraro shot back, "Are you saying that I would have to have fought in a war in order to love peace? . . . When we stop the arms race, we make this a safer, saner world, and that's a patriotic act. And when we keep the peace, young men don't die, and that's a patriotic act." In her book, *Ferraro, My Story,* she stressed that "the most important issue as a leader . . . was to do everything possible not to get to the point of having to decide whether to use force."[2]

In the end, the Mondale-Ferraro ticket lost. But their campaign was said to have opened doors for women. While the possibility of electing women to prominent positions opened up, however, the numbers of women actually able to win them are few. By 1995, ten years after Mondale and Ferraro's campaign, there were more women in Congress than at any other time in history, but they still made up only 11 percent of the total membership. Their ranks among the top leadership posts are dismal and they must still fight very hard for each small victory.

Still, these numbers didn't deter Ferraro from public office. She ran for a U.S. Senate seat in 1992. The primary contest was a difficult one and Ferraro lost her bid to become the first female senator from New York. After that race, Ferraro joined a New York law firm and seemed to have taken a break from the world of politics. But in 1996, her name surfaced

Geraldine Ferraro at the Democratic National Convention in 1984 accepting the vice presidential nomination

again when she began considering a run for mayor of New York City or governor of New York state. She explained, "Those are the positions with real ability to get things done."[3]

8

Women in the Senate

When Jeannette Rankin joined Congress in 1917, the world looked upon her as an oddity, a woman out of place in the man's world of politics. By 1992, when one election brought four women to the U.S. Senate, women were no longer considered an oddity. Rather, they were looked upon with great expectation and admiration. Americans expected them to be leaders and active players in directing the country. But the women in the U.S. Senate today—indeed women across the country—owe much to their foremothers who struggled to earn such respect.

Hattie Caraway

Rebecca Felton's name may be the first female name on the rolls of the U.S. Senate, but the first woman

Senator Barbara Mikulski (right) advising newly elected senators Carol Moseley Braun, Patty Murray, and Barbara Boxer in November 1992

senator elected in her own right was Hattie Caraway (D–Ark.; sen. 1931–45). Caraway didn't particularly want the job, but when her husband Thaddeus died in 1931 with a year still left in his senatorial term, she won the spot in a special election. The politicians back home were pleased with her unopposed run. This gave them time to maneuver and select a male candidate to run in the general election.

What these men didn't count on was Senator Caraway's quiet ways. Dubbed "Silent Hattie" because she rarely spoke during Senate debates, she greatly appreciated the power and symbolism of a Senate seat. Six men had declared their intentions to run for that seat in 1932. With just a short time before the election, Caraway joined the roster. No one thought she had much of a chance except for another senator, Huey Long, a Democrat from Louisiana.

Senator Long was known as "Kingfish" and fashioned himself as a leader of the underdog, a populist who said he would fight for "everyman." Long had come to admire Caraway's quiet demeanor. Her voting record and opinions on issues like tax reform and improving the financial opportunities for the common person mirrored Long's. When Long took it upon himself to fashion Caraway's campaign, he saw a chance to spread his own message in the South. Caraway's home state of Arkansas presented a good opportunity to widen his base of support in preparation for a presidential run he was considering.

Senator Long had a unique campaign style—part politics, part circus. As a campaigner, Long traveled with a well-oiled machine of supporters who made each rally a major event. His sideshow included campaign stops in as many counties as possible throughout the state. At each stop the show would begin with men handing out pamphlets and information, then watching the crowd for any disruptions. His skill at

Hattie Caraway, who rode along on Huey Long's coattails to reelection, became an influential speaker and popular senator. In 1941 she spoke on revisions to the U.S. Neutrality Act during World War II.

manipulating the emotions of a crowd was legendary. When Senator Long sang the praises of Hattie Caraway with the charisma and charm of a revival preacher, "Silent Hattie" suddenly found a voice. And a convincing voice it was. Hattie Caraway walked away with almost as many votes as her six competitors together. She became the first woman to win a Senate seat by popular vote.

Senator Long's style and his crafty strategies leading to the White House were not so popular. Long was assassinated in 1935. Senator Caraway persevered without her mentor. She won reelection in 1938. Her focus had always been the same as her husband's. In fact, again and again Senator Caraway reminded the voters and her colleagues that she was in Washington to carry on Thad's work. She was appointed to the Agriculture and Forestry Committee and the Commerce Committee. This allowed her to have a say in farming legislation and other programs that would ease the burden of her constituents—rural farmers and their families suffering through the Depression.

She remained true to her husband's values but had a style all her own. Often she would sit quietly in the Senate chamber knitting while the men debated. When asked about this, she once replied, "It's funny how they all talk on after we [women] have made up our minds."

Senator Caraway remained in the Senate thirteen years. She was finally unseated in 1944 by J. William Fulbright (who served several successive terms himself). She remained in Washington, and President Truman appointed her to the Employees' Compensation Commission. She died in 1950, leaving a legacy for the eighteen women who followed her to the Senate.

Reluctant Leaders

The years from Silent Hattie's service to the late 1970s saw the election or appointment of only nine more women to the Senate. Several found themselves there because of the "Widow's Mandate." Conventional wisdom said that wives should go to Washington to do what their husbands would have done. The problem was that the life of a politician was not what most of these wives had imagined for themselves. The women who chose to run for office during these years invariably did so because their husbands had died or because they were willing to fill a gap until a general election could be held. But without fail, these women approached the Senate with respect and with a commitment to do the best job they could.

Rose McConnell Long (D–La.; sen. 1936), the wife of Democratic Senator Huey Long, was the natural choice of Louisiana's governor to fill the Senate seat when Long was assassinated in late 1935. By January 1936, Rose Long had been sworn in at the U.S. Senate. Although not as charismatic or as loud as her husband, Senator Long did serve a distinguished year, putting much of her energy into securing assistance and support for Louisiana. She left Washington almost a year to the day after she arrived.

Although their terms were separated by thirty-three years, Democrats **Dixie Bibb Graves** (D–Ala.; sen. 1938–39) and **Elaine Edwards** (D–La.; sen. 1972) shared the same circumstances in becoming senators. Both were appointed by their governor husbands and both did exactly what was expected of them.

Governor Bibb Graves of Alabama faced the prospect of appointing someone to fill a Senate seat vacated by Hugo Black in 1937. Black was leaving to join the Supreme Court. Back in Alabama, Governor Graves decided to appoint his wife, Dixie, though she had little experience or interest in politics. This was an easy choice for him. It meant that Graves didn't have to choose someone from the long list of qualified politicians, some of whom were his friends and allies. It also meant he could be sure that Dixie Graves would not seek another term. He expected her to leave the seat open for the man who could win the upcoming election.

The governor's decision met with much animosity. The qualified male candidates were angry that they had been outmaneuvered, and women were angry because the appointment of an unqualified woman made a mockery of women in politics. But Dixie Bibb Graves was not entirely unqualified. She had come from a political family and helped her husband's campaign. It was not uncommon for Mrs. Graves to give speeches when her husband couldn't be in attendance. Rumor has it she even wrote some of his speeches.

Dixie Graves spent six months in the Senate and earned a reputation as an apt politician. She had won so many hearts that some Alabamans wanted her to run for the next full term. She did not. After five months in office, she went back to the life she had led.

Elaine Edwards's story is almost identical. Her husband, the governor of Louisiana, appointed her to fill an unexpired term in August 1972. His decision was based on the knowledge that his wife would not seek another term or use the office for her personal gain. It was clear, however, that he intended his wife to use the office for *his* personal gain.

Senator Edwards would have preferred staying home with her four children, but she stoically played a part in her husband's plan. She made little effort to disguise the fact that she consulted Governor Edwards on almost every vote. Her defense of this practice was that she and her husband both wanted what was best for Louisiana.

The feminists of the day were angry. They promoted the same argument as their foremothers did with Dixie Graves: Why mock women's talent and drive for politics by appointing a women who had neither? During her three months in office, Senator Edwards did little to answer the criticism. Though she didn't speak on the Senate floor, she was active on her committees and managed to secure some patronage for Louisiana. She resigned in November of the same year to return to her role as wife and mother.

The first Republican woman senator was **Gladys Pyle** (R–S.D.; sen. 1938–39). Her victory in a special election was really an empty gesture. She was elected in November 1938 and her term expired in January 1939. Since Congress was not in session, she never even spoke on the Senate floor. But Senator Pyle was not a pawn in someone else's game. Rather, she was a politician who saw the opportunity to make a point and establish a presence. Pyle remained active all her life and believed it was every citizen's duty to participate in politics. She learned this lesson from her mother, Mamie Shields Pyle, a leader in the suffrage movement in South Dakota.

In 1921, at the age of thirty-two, Gladys Pyle was elected to the South Dakota State Legislature and served for two terms. She then became secretary of state and, later, the winner of a primary election for governor. She was active in the Republican Party and in 1940 was selected to give the nominating speech when her state delegation placed its own candidate for the party's presidential nomination.

About ten years later, South Dakota had another Republican woman senator who didn't even travel to Washington. **Vera Bushfield** (R–S.D.; sen. 1948–49) was appointed to fill her husband's seat after he died in October 1948. As the governor made the announcement, he made a point of saying that Vera Bushfield was being appointed with the understanding that she resign after the upcoming November election.

Bushfield still called it an honor and spent her brief time as a senator attending to the needs and requests of her constituents. Instead of going to Washington she remained close to her neighbors and did what she could, knowing that Congress was not even in session.

The November election sent a man to fill the Senate seat, and Vera Bushfield returned her attentions to her family. Many years after her brief senatorial experience, Bushfield, at age eighty, spoke eloquently on the importance of women's continued growth in politics:

> *As for a woman making a career of politics, we have had proof that congresswomen have done much to demonstrate they are as capable of holding office as most men. On many occasions a woman is more conscious of the pulse of the people than a man. She has a better understanding of what life in the home is like. She is closer to the youth. With intelligence and effort, she can easily learn the fundamentals of government, especially nowadays when education is available to anyone who has the ambition to pursue it. More than ever the political odds are in a woman's favor.*[1]

Eva Bowring (R–Nebr.; sen. 1954) and **Hazel Abel** (R–Nebr.; sen. 1954–55), became the first two women from the same state to become senators in succession. Bowring was appointed in April 1954 to fill a six-month vacancy. Abel then won a special election in November of the same year to serve just two months in the Senate. Both women shared a background in politics and in running their husbands' businesses as widows. Each was known for her good humor and good sense. Senator Bowring spoke on the Senate floor in defense of farmers, and Senator Abel cast a difficult vote to censure Senator Joseph McCarthy.

Maurine Neuberger (D–Oreg.; sen. 1961–67) became a widow two days before the deadline to file for a Senate election in 1960. Her husband was the well-known and well-respected Oregon Democratic Senator Dick Neuberger.

The simultaneous tragedy and opportunity created a crisis for Maurine Neuberger. They were both popular politicians—she served two terms in the Oregon House while her husband was in the state Senate—and she knew the voters would not begrudge her filling her husband's place. But she wanted to win the seat on her own merits.

Neuberger beat out four challengers in the primary election and continued on to victory in the general election. During her six-year term, Senator Neuberger was not shy. She spoke out often on issues of importance to herself and to Oregon. She cosponsored a truth-in-packaging bill mandating that cosmetics makers list product ingredients on their packages. She also began an antismoking campaign and wrote a book on the subject, *Smoke Screen: Tobacco and the Public Welfare*. During her last year in office, she held a series of hearings as chair of a subcommittee of the Special Committee on Aging.

Senator Neuberger decided not to run for reelection. She had remarried and moved to the east coast, where she continued on as chair of the Citizens' Advisory council on the Status of Women.

Nancy Landon Kassebaum

In 1937, just seventeen years after women won the right to vote, Senator Hattie Caraway looked on as Dixie Graves was sworn in. Two women were serving concurrently in the Senate. For five years after that, Senator Margaret Chase Smith was the sole female vote, until Senators Bowring and Abel joined her for a short time. After Senator Nancy Kassebaum (R–Kans.; sen. 1978–97) was elected in 1978, she, too, became the single female vote in the "most exclusive gentle-

Nancy Kassebaum met with President Ronald Reagan in 1981 to express her support for a controversial plan to sell AWACS (Airborne Warning and Control Systems) surveillance planes to Saudi Arabia.

man's club" in America. In many ways Kassebaum brought the new style of female activism and career politics to the Senate. She joined the growing roster of women who had achieved some of their political goals in the House, but she was one of few who reached the Senate.

As political families go, the Landons of Kansas ranked among the most well-known. Alf Landon ran for U.S. President against Franklin D. Roosevelt in 1936. He lost by an embarrassing margin. Nevertheless, the Landon home was always known as a political one, and the family enjoyed a great deal of popularity in Kansas politics. So it was no surprise that in 1978, when Alf Landon's daughter, Nancy Landon Kassebaum, decided to run for the U.S. Senate, the Landon name helped Kassebaum beat out eight other Republican candidates in a heated primary race.

Nancy Kassebaum did not fit the profile of the other women politicians in the 1970s. Shirley Chisholm, Elizabeth Holtzman, and Bella Abzug all came to politics after many years of activism and holding elective office in their own states. Even though Kassebaum had been raised in a political family, she did not choose to become active in politics until later in life. She had studied political science in college, but when she married Phillip Kassebaum she put aside any aspirations she may have had in order to raise a family. She was involved in her community of Maize, a small town just outside Wichita, Kansas.

In 1975 however, Kassebaum's life changed. She separated from her husband and decided to take a job in Washington, D.C., working for James Pearson, a senator from Kansas. A few years later, when Pearson announced that he would not to run for reelection, Kassebaum weighed the odds and decided to run for his seat. Her divorce had been finalized and her four children were older. The time was right for Nancy Kassebaum to run for the Senate.

In a field of nine men and two women running for the Republican nomination, Kassebaum had no trouble sticking out. The Landon name took her far and her family money helped her buy much-needed advertising. But she didn't take the easy road and insisted on speaking her mind even when her views were unpopular.

In 1973, the Supreme Court upheld a woman's right to choose a safe and legal abortion in the famous

Roe v. Wade case. Five years later the country was still at odds over the issue, and Kassebaum's views on abortion became an important issue in the 1978 race. She has always believed in a woman's right to choose. This was not a popularly held view in Kansas and Kassebaum knew it. Still, when asked, she addressed the issue in a straightforward and honest manner. It was this straightforwardness (and the Landon name) that helped her become the first woman ever elected to the United States Senate who had not followed her husband or had been drafted by party leaders to "save a seat." (Hattie Caraway was elected in her own right but only after completing the term of her deceased husband, and Margaret Chase Smith was first elected to Congress in her husband's stead.)

As the only woman in the Senate in 1979, Senator Kassebaum was immediately pegged as a spokeswoman for all of America's women. This was not a job she relished or embraced, as did Bella Abzug and Shirley Chisholm. Senator Kassebaum went to Washington as the representative for Kansas. Yet she was very clear about her belief in equal rights and equal responsibilities. For instance, Senator Kassebaum supported the idea of the Equal Rights Amendment, but she also supported a bill requiring women to be drafted into national service just like men. She joined the Congressional Caucus for Women's Issues but never became a very active member. This was in large part because the majority of the members were Democrats.

Her positions on abortion and on women's rights were not always in line with the Republican Party. In fact, after Republican Ronald Reagan was elected president in 1980 and the Republicans gained control of the Senate, Kassebaum found herself at odds with her party's leaders. She often disagreed with the Reagan administration on foreign policy decisions. On social issues, Senator Kassebaum was known for being more moderate than her colleagues and certainly more moderate than the presidential administration.

Still, as one of two women in the Senate (Paula Hawkins, a Florida Republican, was elected in 1980), Kassebaum was in the enviable position of assuming leadership roles mainly because she was a woman. But this prize came with some strings attached. Two women and ninety-eight men meant the Senate was still an "all men's club," and it was often left to Senator Kassebaum to point out the subtle inequities she faced. At a party gathering she was once introduced by the music of "Ain't She Sweet," a reference to her gender and her petite build. The song is about admiring a woman for her physique as she walks down the street. Hardly appropriate for a powerful politician!

Over the years, Kassebaum overcame the initial jokes and presumptions of her ability. She easily won reelection twice and became a very popular junior senator. She was only the second woman to be a committee chair (Hattie Caraway was the first). She led the Labor and Human Resources Committee and pursued her interest in foreign affairs by serving on the Senate Committee on Foreign Relations for fifteen years. She supported a bill that imposed economic sanctions against South Africa for its apartheid policies and spent many years advocating assistance for famine-plagued parts of Africa.

In the 104th Congress, which convened in 1995, Senator Kassebaum was an important player, respected by colleagues on both sides of the aisle. In a congressional session marked by intense partisanship, Kassebaum built coalitions and consensus. She was also very concerned that Senate rules not be abused for political gain. For instance, during her first term she supported the Equal Rights Amendment but did not agree with a parliamentary procedure that prolonged the period allowed for ratification.

While a true Republican, Kassebaum had no qualms about disagreeing with her party's leaders when she felt it was necessary. In 1995 she did not support the confirmation of Henry Foster for surgeon general, but she wouldn't go along with her party's plan for a filibuster to delay a vote on the nomination. In another touchy issue, she broke with her party to support President Clinton's crime bill, which was opposed by the Republican Party, largely because of its gun restrictions. Unlike many of her colleagues, Kassebaum openly criticized the National Rifle Association (NRA). This is a courageous position, because the NRA gives a lot of money to candidates who support them. It also can muster strong lobbying efforts.

Taking a moderate position on issues doesn't always make for interesting headlines. Still, Senator Kassebaum maintained a clear view of her role as politician. She enjoyed trying to figure out legislative answers without demeaning the government in which she served. Her respect, from men and women, Republicans and Democrats, reflected her success in this process. She announced her intention to resign from the Senate after her term expires in 1997.

Paula Hawkins

It didn't take long for Senator Paula Hawkins (R–Fla.; sen. 1980-87) to make a reputation for herself. The problem was that it was a reputation few would savor. In an effort to make a strong statement against people who cheated the food stamp program (designed to provide assistance for people who couldn't afford groceries), Senator Hawkins announced her plan for mandatory imprisonment for those cheaters. But she made the announcement at a swank luncheon where guests were served an expensive meal of sirloin steak.

It didn't end there. After her "steak and jail" lunch, Hawkins angered her Florida colleagues by taking credit for a series of federal projects that would benefit the state. It had been a joint effort among all of Florida's representatives, but Senator Hawkins managed to get all the publicity. If this wasn't enough of a bad start to a senatorial term, Senator Hawkins began to suffer from migraines and backaches after a television studio backdrop fell on her during a taping.

But politicians almost always have the opportunity for redemption. In 1984, Senator Hawkins shared a very personal story with the public; she had been sexually molested as a child. It was a secret she carried with her for decades. Her husband didn't even know. But when she began working with a social worker on a piece of legislation, Senator Hawkins realized the need to go public with her story.

In 1984 there were few organizations focused on the victims of sexual abuse. Immediately Senator Hawkins's revelation got a response. She was swept away in a series of interviews and public speeches. She was credited with giving a face to the problem of child abuse and for increasing public awareness and public action. A year later, Senator Hawkins published a book called *Children at Risk*. In it, she discusses the need for personal and legislative action to combat the horrors of sexual abuse.

Children's issues had always been a focus for Senator Hawkins. She was the author of the Missing Children Act of 1982 which established a system for finding missing children.

Hawkins also focused on narcotics control, a big problem for Florida. She founded the Senate Drug Enforcement Caucus and worked to pressure the governments of drug-trafficking countries to crack down on the problem. In 1984 the Senate unanimously approved an amendment by Hawkins to cut off foreign aid to any country that did not reduce the amount of drugs that got through to the United States.

Senator Hawkins usually voted with a block of politicians called the "New Right." She opposed the Equal Rights Amendment and supported prayer in public schools. But when an issue directly affected her constituency, she voted in their best interests. For instance, Florida is home to many retired people who depend on Social Security benefits. In 1985, near the end of her first term, Senator Hawkins broke rank and voted against President Ronald Reagan's plan to limit Social Security increases.

It had taken two tries before Paula Hawkins won her seat in the Senate. But her time in Washington was limited to just one term. She lost her bid for six more years in the Senate to Florida's governor, Democrat Bob Graham. The two engaged in a tight race. Senator Hawkins had managed to win over many supporters because of the emotional issues she sought to publicize. But Governor Graham was popular. Both candidates put up a good fight but Hawkins lost the race. She garnered 45 percent of the vote compared to Graham's 55 percent.

Barbara Mikulski

Although Republican Nancy Kassebaum was in the Senate many years, it is Barbara Mikulski (D–Md.; rep. 1977–86, sen. 1986–) who has become known as the Dean of Women in the U.S. Senate. After 1992 Senator Mikulski held a special place as the leader of the other four Democratic women senators—Feinstein, Boxer, Braun, and Murray.

She became a senator in the same way as many of the women in Congress today. As she herself explains, "Most of the women that hold public office essentially . . . don't come through the traditional routes of being in a nice law firm or belonging to the right club . . . but go into politics because they see a wrong they want to right or a need that must be filled."[2] In her case, Mikulski, then a social worker, organized a grassroots coalition of African-Americans, Poles, and other ethnic groups to oppose the construction of a freeway through their neighborhoods. The coalition was successful, and Mikulski was on her way to being known as a true leader of the people of Maryland.

Mikulski is proud of her Polish heritage and fits right in with the ethnic communities in and around Baltimore. Her parents taught her the importance of people looking out for one another, for their friends and neighbors. After strengthening her political philosophies, Mikulski looked at politics with a more serious eye.

She was first elected to the Baltimore City Council in 1971, a seat she held for five years. She also continued to be active in other groups and in fighting for women's rights. Her first try for the U.S. House of Representatives was in 1974. She lost to the GOP challenger by a slim margin. She tried again in 1976 when a well-liked congressman was leaving the House for the Senate. Mikulski saw her chance. She won that election and stayed in the House of Representatives with wide voter support for ten years.

Representative Mikulski was successful in protecting the interests of Maryland and of the many ethnic groups she represented. She was also well liked by women's groups and proudly calls herself a feminist. She has continually fought to preserve a woman's right to choose an abortion and is a tireless advocate

Barbara Mikulski in 1986, when she was in the House of Representatives

for women's health issues. Representative Mikulski was also instrumental in winning financial support for the National Science Foundation. When her colleagues in the House—Holtzman, Heckler, and Chisholm—took up the reins to create the Congresswomen's Caucus, Mikulski joined the group and was instrumental in its formation.

When one of Maryland's senators retired, Mikulski saw her opportunity to enter the Senate. Her outspoken style, her sense of humor, her grasp of the issues, and her success in the House all contributed to a resounding win. Another contributing factor was money. For the first time, women were banding together and pooling their money. A new organization called EMILY's List was formed. EMILY—Early Money Is Like Yeast (that is, it makes things grow)—contributed more than $250,000 to Mikulski's campaign. This organization is dedicated to helping Democratic women candidates. A similar organization, called WISH (Women In the Senate and House), was founded for Republican women.

In 1986, at the age of fifty, Barbara Mikulski joined the ranks of Hattie Caraway and Maurine Neuberger as a Democratic woman senator. The Senate's only unabashed feminist, Senator Mikulski is always outspoken with her views on issues of importance to women. She works closely with the Congressional Caucus on Women's Issues. She has always supported the Equal Rights Amendment, pay equity issues, and a woman's right to choose an abortion. The responsibility of being a woman in the Senate in not lost on her. She said, "You feel that you are speaking for every woman in the world who has ever lived in the past, who currently lives today, and who will live into the third millennium."[3]

Her candid talk and sincerity has won her many fans. She holds powerful junior leadership positions, including Assistant Floor Leader for the Democratic Party. Senator Mikulski also sits on the Ethics Committee. This assignment was no doubt precipitated by the Thomas hearings. Anxious to give the impression of diversity, senators jumped at the chance of finding a woman to serve on this important committee. Soon the Ethics Committee was to show the significance of its task of monitoring the behavior of members of the Senate itself.

The committee was charged with investigating allegations of sexual harassment and other abuses of power by Republican Senator Bob Packwood of Oregon. Senator Packwood was long known as a supporter and advocate of women's issues. He was also well liked and greatly respected by his male colleagues, many of whom had served with him for years.

When allegations of sexual impropriety arose from more than twenty different women, it was a blow to all those who worked with Packwood. In a Republican-controlled Congress, the Ethics Committee was slow to do its work. When it was discovered that Senator Packwood had altered some of his diary entries in an effort to hide other offenses, the Ethics Committee got angry. But even this transgression was not enough to force the committee to conduct public hearings on the matter. Senator Packwood was the chairman of the powerful Senate Finance Committee and was needed to help pass important legislation the Republicans had on their agenda.

Senator Mikulski was outspoken in her assertions that the committee must fully investigate the matter. She was the only committee member to go public with her requests for investigation. She was joined by Senator Barbara Boxer, who was not a member of that committee but is credited with forcing the Senate to vote on whether or not to hold public hearings on this matter. The vote was defeated, along party lines, but it succeeded in bringing the issue into the public spotlight. Eventually, Bob Packwood resigned to avoid continued investigations into the charges.

Situations like the Packwood case can cause one to lose faith in the system or become disheartened. Even in such situations, though, Senator Mikulski remains an advocate for her constituents, a role model for her colleagues in the Senate, and a public servant who still enjoys the job.

1992: The Year of the Woman

THE SO-CALLED "Year of the Woman" produced numerous gains for women in Congress. After elections held in November 1992, forty-seven women were serving in the House and six in the Senate. Patty Murray of Washington, Barbara Boxer and Dianne Feinstein of California, and Carol Moseley Braun of Illinois all joined the Senate for the 103rd Congress. (Nancy Kassebaum and Barbara Mikulski were already in the Senate.) But their victories were tempered by reality. In one instance, when Braun went to get her picture taken for a Capitol Hill photo ID, the card she got back listed her as "Spouse" instead of "Senator." Without losing her sense of humor, Senator Braun suggested that the clerk try again.

Presidential candidate Bill Clinton campaigned in California with Senate candidates Dianne Feinstein and Barbara Boxer in October 1992. All three won, and California was the first state to send two women to the Senate at the same time.

Anita Hill and the Senate Judiciary Committee

A good sense of humor is vital in politics—but so is a good dose of anger. The spectacle of Anita Hill being interrogated by an all-white, all-male Judiciary Committee enraged the nation's women. Clarence Thomas, an African-American, was actually the one for whom the hearings were held. He had been nominated by President George Bush to become a Supreme Court justice. On the surface, Thomas had a reputable career as a lawyer, lower court judge, and head of the Equal Employment Opportunity Commission (EEOC)—a government department that investigates allegations of discrimination in hiring, firing, or workplace conditions.

Questions began to arise when Thomas was noncommittal about his stance on abortion rights and told the committee (and the nation via televised hearings) that he had never discussed the issue during law school or after. This made many feminists skeptical. Abortion had become a litmus test of sorts to gauge where a judge or candidate sat on the liberal/conservative spectrum. Many people assume that liberals support a woman's right to choose a safe and legal abortion while conservatives will support the rights of an unborn child. This is, of course, a simplified way to label political views. There are certainly other ways to determine a person's political position. And there are times—especially when choosing a Supreme Court justice—when we are not supposed to base our opinions on an individual's political leanings.

In the court of public opinion, people often will not delve much below the surface of a candidate. They find it easier to form their opinions based on a fact/belief or two. In the case of Clarence Thomas, his unknown stance on abortion was not enough to disqualify him from serving on the highest court in the nation. But it did raise some red flags because of his reply that he never discussed it.

What happened next riveted the country and divided friends, neighbors, and families. A law professor from Oklahoma named Anita Hill came forward with allegations of sexual harassment against Thomas. The Senate chose to ignore her remarks and tried to rush through the rest of the hearings. But in a highly publicized event, on October 8, 1991, Pat Schroeder led a contingent of female representatives—Barbara Boxer, Eleanor Holmes Norton, Louise M. Slaughter, Jolene Unsoeld, Nita Lowey, and Patsy Mink—on a short march from the House floor to the Senate side of the Capitol. Amid blazing flashbulbs, they were there to ask their colleagues in the Senate Democratic Caucus to at least listen to Anita Hill. The all-male Caucus refused to let the women in until the threat of reporters and photographers hungry for a story made them reconsider.

Soon Hill found herself in the same committee hearing room as Thomas, facing the panel of white male senators and testifying that she had been sexually harassed by Clarence Thomas. The two had worked together at the EEOC, and Hill, also African-American, recounted Thomas's subtle remarks and adolescent tricks. The white men on the panel, U.S. senators from both parties, transformed the hearings and essentially put Hill on trial. Their questions, assumptions, and condescending language were nothing new to millions of women who had already heard these words from male bosses and coworkers.

But this was something different. For the first time in anyone's memory, a woman was publicly saying that this type of behavior—which American women have endured for centuries—was inappropriate

Anita Hill took the oath in October 1991 and testified before the Senate Judiciary Committee that Supreme Court nominee Clarence Thomas had sexually harassed her. The questioning of Hill by the committee became so intense that it seemed Hill herself was on trial.

and unfair. Hill's testimony sent the message that a man waiting to be confirmed to serve on the highest court in the land should know better and have more respect for women. In some now-famous exchanges, Senator Arlen Specter said Hill was just plain lying; Senator Orrin Hatch said Hill found her ideas and "wanton ways" in pornographic books; and the whole committee just seemed to assume that she was either jealous of Thomas's success or angry because Thomas didn't return her affection.

Across the country, people were asked, "Who do you believe?" Polls indicated some surprising results. Not all women by any means sided with Hill and not all men with Thomas. What seemed to be a major factor in the debate was race. Hill and Thomas are both black, the committee members were all white. Some people in the African-American community saw this as airing their dirty laundry in public, thinking Hill should have kept quiet so that a black man could serve on the Supreme Court. He may not be perfect, but without him, the Court would be composed of only white judges. (He was nominated to replace Thurgood Marshall, the only other black Supreme Court justice.)

In the end, after horrible things were said and printed about both Thomas and Hill, the Senate confirmed the nominee by a vote of 52–48, the smallest of margins (and not strictly along party lines). But the tempest had only begun.

The Thomas-Hill hearings (as they were called, making it seem that Hill was on trial, too) became a rallying point for women politicians. It had never been clearer that more women were needed in Congress. The Judiciary Committee and their treatment of Anita Hill made it plain as day that women were being kept out of important leadership positions—namely the U.S. Senate.

With elections just a year away, women mobilized, and some who had never considered running for such high office found themselves on the campaign trail. Patty Murray became "a mom in tennis shoes," Carol Moseley Braun campaigned to be the first African-American woman in the Senate, and California had the potential to send two women to the Senate, Barbara Boxer and Dianne Feinstein.

These four women, who all won their elections, bore striking similarities to one another but embodied vast differences. Although they campaigned as outsiders to the "Senate gentleman's club," all of these women had been active politicians for many years before seeking higher office.

Patty Murray

After an opponent referred to her as just "a mom in tennis shoes," Patty Murray (D–Wash.; sen. 1992–) realized that she was exactly that. She saw this as a quality that made her qualified to go to Washington, D.C., to speak for all the other moms and dads in tennis shoes struggling to raise families. Her campaign for the Senate in 1992 was filled with references to being an outsider. She portrayed herself as a working mother who was more representative of her state than those men "in gray suits and red ties," as she called them.

Even though she campaigned as a newcomer to politics, Murray had actually served her constituency as a school board member for six years and then as a state senator from 1989 to her election to the U.S. Senate. Like many women in politics, Murray became involved when an issue close to home grabbed her attention and spurred her to action. In 1979 she organized twelve thousand families to fight to save a preschool program that was threatened with extinc-

Senator Patty Murray brought her daughter Sarah to work with her in April 1993 as part of the "Take Our Daughters to Work" campaign. During the Senate race Murray's opposition called her "a mom in tennis shoes." She turned that accusation to her advantage by speaking on behalf of working parents and struggling families.

tion. At first the legislators in power didn't fear much from this mom, but Murray soon showed she was tougher than anyone expected.

Along with Senator Barbara Boxer from California, Senator Murray is an outspoken opponent of sexual harassment in all its forms, especially when it hits the Senate. In fact, a stroke of ironic luck helped Murray during the election. She would have faced the incumbent senator, Brock Adams, but he dropped out of the race only after a newspaper publicized that eight women had accused him of sexual advances and impropriety. Imagine this happening when the Thomas-Hill debacle was still ringing in the voters' ears!

Taking this one step further, Murray continued to remind voters that the problem was not just limited to Thomas and Brock but to the archaic attitude of the Senate as a whole. With so few women's voices the Senate was, indeed, still a men's club. But this powerful club was deciding issues that affect each of us every day. After a difficult primary and challenging general election, Murray beat her GOP opponent, Rod Chandler, by a wide margin.

During her time in Congress, Murray has been an active participant. She is interested in the daily challenges faced by working parents. She has called for a clear sexual harassment policy to be enacted in the Senate. (She had written one for the Washington State Legislature a few years earlier.) She also protested vehemently when a high-ranking Navy admiral, accused of sexual harassment, was about to retire with the consent of the Senate and a very large pension.

Murray is one of several members of Congress who must balance environmental concerns with economic ones. In her home state of Washington, logging and salmon fishing are very large and important industries employing thousands of people. Many say these industries are problematic because they take precious resources from the earth without replenishing them. To face these problems, Murray sponsored legislation to ban the export of logs taken from public lands while also supporting bills that would help the economically ailing timber industry.

Murray has proven herself a very able politician willing to play along with the leadership while retaining her individuality and independence. In many respects her approach to politics on Capitol Hill is similar to that of her colleague, Senator Barbara Boxer of California.

Barbara Boxer

Barbara Boxer (D–Calif.; rep. 1983–93, sen. 1992-) fully recognizes her place in history. In her semi-autobiographical book, *Strangers in the Senate: Politics and the New Revolution of Women in America*, Boxer provides a brief overview of women senators who have come before her. Boxer also recognizes that what she may not be able to do alone could be done with the cooperation of the other female senators serving with her. On more than one occasion Boxer has rallied these senators to attack an issue. Perhaps she learned this lesson when she joined Pat Schroeder and five other women from the House in a march over to the Senate to protest the handling of Anita Hill's allegations against Supreme Court nominee Clarence Thomas. But throughout her long political career, Boxer has learned the importance of building coalitions.

Boxer first ran for public office in 1972. Her husband was considering a run for the Board of Supervisors of Marin County, California, but suggested that his wife run instead. The reason? He would have looked like all the other candidates, but Barbara would stand out. Boxer recounts the attitudes of family, friends, and strangers alike—men and women—who wondered why on earth she would want to run for office. Boxer's answer—that she didn't want to sit on the sidelines while the country fought a war in Vietnam, and that she worried about the future her children would face—didn't seem to bring in the votes. She lost the race.

But Boxer ran again and won, serving on the Board of Supervisors from 1977 to 1983. From there she made the jump to the U.S. House of Representatives, where she served five terms. In the House, Boxer developed a reputation for being aggressive on the issues yet managing to get along with her colleagues, whether or not they agreed with her. Her liberal agenda included strong support for abortion rights, gay and lesbian rights, and issues facing women and families. But it was her determination to reduce the defense budget that gained her the greatest publicity of her years in the House.

During her first year in Congress, Boxer learned that a part made for military planes—a small metal object that had no direct function in the flying of the plane or in communications—cost $850. This was enough to set her off, and she immediately took on the military and the Reagan Administration. This was a gutsy thing for a freshman member of Congress, and even gutsier when you consider the support for military buildups that occurred during Reagan's presidency. After much publicity Boxer passed legislation that forced more competition among those bidding for defense contracts. It wasn't that she did not appreciate a strong military, but rather that she was very concerned about the nation's spending and budget deficit.

As a senator, Boxer again made headlines and ran afoul of Congress. Unfortunately, the subject had returned to sexual harassment. A colleague, Oregon Republican Senator Bob Packwood, was accused of unwanted sexual advances by almost twenty different women over a period of many years. (Prior to these allegations, Senator Packwood was considered an ardent supporter of women's issues.) Following its rigid internal-rule system, the Senate brought the case before its own Ethics Committee. After months and months of investigation and ample evidence of wrongdoing, the Ethics Panel voted to keep the testimony of these women closed so that the public could not witness it. This enraged the women of the Senate—most of whom are there because of their rage at similar treatment of Anita Hill's allegations.

The full Senate was forced to vote on whether or not to open up the Packwood hearings only because Boxer waged a one-woman war to get this issue out to the public. Not surprisingly, the overwhelmingly male Senate voted to keep the doors closed. (Packwood eventually resigned.) But despite this outcome, Boxer remains a tireless worker ready to speak her truths to the public.

Dianne Feinstein

In 1978 national attention was paid to Dianne Feinstein (D–Calif.; sen. 1992–), then the president of the San Francisco Board of Supervisors. She had just become acting mayor after the shooting deaths of Mayor George Moscone and Supervisor Harvey Milk. Both men had been murdered by another supervisor, Dan White. As she was led to a microphone to announce the tragedy, blood still on her skirt, Feinstein managed to calm the shocked city with a strong, soothing tone of voice. She promised the people, "As we reconstructed the city after the physical damage done by an earthquake and fire, so too can we rebuild from the spiritual damage." As San Francisco mayor for the next ten years, Dianne Feinstein indeed led the city out of its pain and into an age of growth. She balanced the city budget, dusted off the famed cable cars, and even brought the National Democratic Convention to her city in 1984.

Feinstein had been interested in politics for many years and first joined the city's Board of Supervisors in 1970. After announcing her decision to run for the position, she was told that the board already had a woman! Undeterred, she ran and won by a huge margin. Two years later she ran for mayor and lost. She'd been a long shot against the very popular incumbent, Joe Alioto. But Feinstein wanted to challenge him, because he was a "machine" politician supported by backroom deals in the Democratic Party—he was doing little to improve the city. She tried again for mayor in 1975 but lost to George Moscone, who had the backing of San Francisco's powerful gay community.

In the 1970s Feinstein dealt with personal tragedy. Her second husband, Bertraum Feinstein, was dying of cancer. (She has a daughter from her first marriage in 1956. The couple divorced soon after that.) Her energy and spirit depleted, Dianne Feinstein decided she didn't want to continue in politics. But that day in front of the microphone in 1978 changed her plans. In a moment she had become mayor of San Francisco—a major political player. In fact, after a decade as mayor, she decided to run for governor against Republican Pete Wilson, a state senator. Feinstein lost this bitter race in 1990, but she stayed in the game.

When Wilson gave up his Senate seat to run for governor, the seat was given to a man named John Seymour until a special election could be held. In that 1992 election, Dianne Feinstein beat Seymour and served the last two years of Wilson's term. The seat came up for election again in 1994 and Feinstein ran with vigor. She had become a popular senator, winning important environmental and economic gains for California. But a Republican millionaire named Michael Huffington decided to run against her. Using his own fortune and a great deal of advertising, Huffington ran a tough campaign. Feinstein defeated him by more than 165,000 votes, but he refused to concede. The fight lasted from November 1994 until February 1995—after the 104th Congress had already convened—before Huffington finally admitted defeat.

Senator Feinstein is known as both liberal and conservative. She supports a woman's right to choose an abortion but advocates for the death penalty. She is an avid supporter of gun control and an environmental crusader. She supported Democratic President Clinton's crime bill, but her stance on the death penalty runs alongside a lot of Republicans. The public's inability to label her one way or the other has often worked in her favor, although it has also prompted many personal attacks.

Whatever one's opinion of Senator Feinstein, she is a savvy politician who has learned her political lessons the hard way. Her skill has not gone unnoticed. Along with Geraldine Ferraro, Feinstein met with presidential candidate Walter Mondale to discuss a possible bid for the vice presidency in 1984. That slot went to Ferraro, but it also put Feinstein squarely on the national political map. Dianne Feinstein continues her tradition of strong leadership and achievement.

Carol Moseley Braun

Exactly twenty-five years after the House of Representatives reluctantly opened its doors to the first African-American woman representative, Shirley Chisholm, the Senate grudgingly did the same. Carol Moseley Braun (D–Ill.; sen. 1992–) became the first black woman senator in 1992. Immediately she was a celebrity, appearing on magazine covers and in gossip columns. Like Chisholm, Braun enjoyed the spotlight, but she was also subjected to investigations into her private life and her handling of campaign finances. Why the scrutiny? It's not that one person is going to change the atmosphere of the whole Senate, but Braun's election and her willingness to speak her mind have made many ponder the effect women have had on the chamber.

Like the other women who ran for the Senate that

year, Braun was deeply affected by the Thomas hearings. She said, "I think people saw the Senate for what it was. They didn't like what they saw. The Senate demystified itself in the eyes of the people."[1] She says that as a young girl she believed she could do what any boy could do. "Racism, sexism, you name the isms, and they're all manifestations of the same evil. I rejected it just as much as I rejected the notion that because I was a girl I couldn't stow away on a tramp steamer if I wanted to, or go explore the Amazon if I wanted to."[2]

Braun came to her Senate seat by way of a career in Illinois politics. The daughter of a Chicago policeman and a medical technician, Braun went to the University of Illinois and got her law degree from the University of Chicago. After spending several years as a federal prosecutor, Braun was elected to the Illinois State Legislature in 1978. She served there more than ten years and rose to a mid-level position of leadership. It was when she was serving as the Cook County Recorder of Deeds that Anita Hill's allegations were front-page news. Braun decided to challenge a popular Illinois senator, Alan Dixon.

In the beginning of the primary election no one took Braun's campaign too seriously. It was a three-way primary, and Dixon was expected to beat both Braun and the other white male challenger. But Braun reminded voters that Dixon had voted to confirm Clarence Thomas. Then a surprising thing happened. A coalition of women and minorities began backing Braun, and each day this group of supporters got bigger. By the time the polls closed, Braun had come up the middle while her two male challengers had split the vote. She had spent a "mere" $400,000, compared to more than $2 million spent by Dixon.

After this victory the ranks of Braun supporters swelled, and the Democratic Party threw its support

Bill Clinton and Al Gore supported Senate candidate Carol Moseley Braun during a rally in Chicago in 1992. Braun won to become the first African-American female senator in American history.

behind her. Her GOP challenger, Rich Williamson, was a man who had served posts in the Reagan administration and walked a straight Republican line. The differences between them were startling, and Braun defeated him easily in the general election. Along the way, Braun's campaign had taken a number of missteps, and she was roasted in the press before she even took office. But after being sworn in on

January 3, 1992, Braun began to live up to the stature of a U.S. senator and has proven to be adept at the work. The first few months in office Braun was constantly in the news as the country looked to her to speak for all women and for all African-Americans—the same expectations placed on Shirley Chisholm twenty-five years earlier.

At this time, Congress was about to grant a congressional patent design to the insignia of the United Daughters of the Confederacy. Braun objected to this because it meant that the Senate would be giving its official sanction to a symbol of the confederacy of states that enslaved African-Americans before the Civil War ended the practice. Braun brought the debate to the Senate floor and reminded the mostly white chamber of growing up in the legacy of slavery and the slap in the face it would be if the Senate sanctioned this insignia.

She won that fight and was praised for her courage and eloquent speech. But not everyone was pleased. In a much publicized event, a Republican senator from North Carolina, Jesse Helms, began singing "Dixie" to Senator Orrin Hatch as they rode in an elevator with Senator Braun. This song has long been a way to refer to the pro-slavery South of the Civil War; it was performed at the inauguration of Jefferson Davis as president of the Confederate States and was a favorite tune of the Confederate Army. Helms is reported as saying, "I'm going to make her cry. I'm going to sing 'Dixie' until she cries." Senator Braun's quick reply was "Senator Helms, your singing would make me cry if you sang 'Rock of Ages.'" (A Helms aide later said it was all meant in good fun.)[3]

Senator Braun understands her place in history but has not lost sight of the job she was sent to do. She wrote, "My presence in and of itself will change the

U.S. Senate. But I cannot do the job that the people of Illinois have asked of me by being a symbol alone."

During her first three years, Braun has proven to be a deft senator. She has waged a war on "deadbeat dads," fathers who do not pay court-ordered child support. She is also very pro-choice and fought along with Barbara Mikulski, Barbara Boxer, and the other women senators to strike down an amendment restricting Medicaid payments for abortion. She served on the Judiciary Committee but was reassigned to the influential Finance Committee in the 104th Congress.

The successes of legislators like Braun, Boxer, Feinstein, and Murray indicate that great change has overtaken Capitol Hill. Although women in Congress still lag behind men in sheer numbers, they have succeeded in refocusing the national political debate to include issues relating directly to women and families.

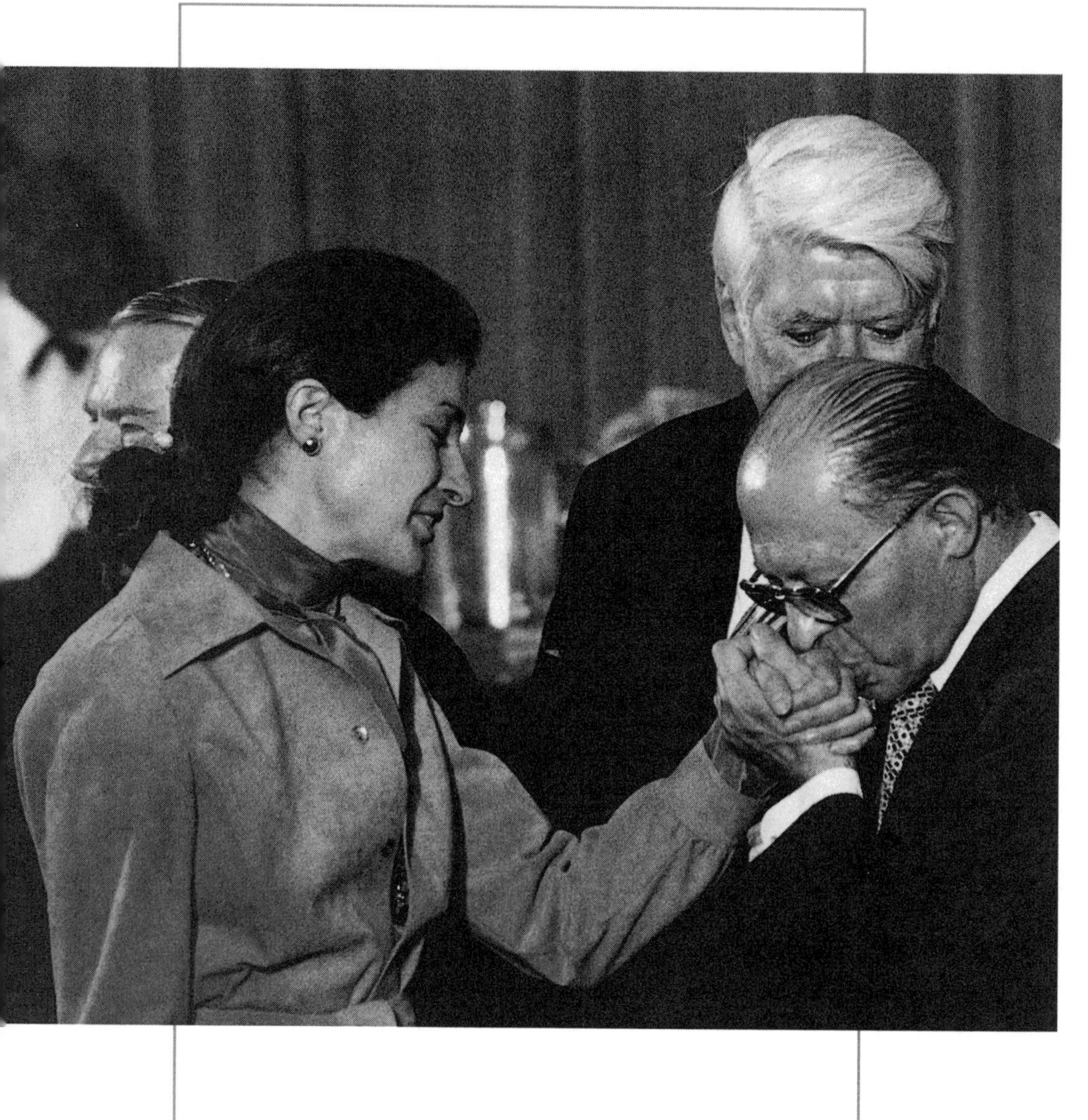

10

Congress Today

After the historic elections of 1992 that sent forty-seven women to the House of Representatives and four new women to the Senate, women in politics were euphoric. It seemed the only way to go was up. They got a surprise in the next elections, held in 1994. This national election did not include the presidency, only members of the House and one-third of the members of the Senate. President Bill Clinton, a Democrat, had spent his first two years in office presiding over a Democratic-controlled Congress. But the voters in 1994 voted many incumbents out of office. For the first time in many years, both houses of Congress had a Republican majority.

Women candidates suffered greatly in this election. Although many women ran for office, their numbers remained stagnant in the next Congress. In 1994 there were still only forty-seven women in the House and only two new women senators, Olympia J. Snowe

Representative Olympia Snowe being greeted by Israeli Prime Minister Menachem Begin in 1979

and Kay Bailey Hutchison, bringing that number up to eight. With the change in majority from Democratic to Republican came a new group of Republican leaders; because of this women have not been very successful in gaining leadership positions or enjoying access to leaders. Still, Snowe and Hutchison are two legislators who enter office already having shown leadership skills in their political careers.

Olympia Snowe

The first Greek-American woman to serve in the Senate, Olympia Snowe (R–Maine; rep. 1979–94, sen. 1994–) was elected in 1994 after serving eight terms in the U.S. House of Representatives. Before that, she had been elected to her late husband's seat in Maine's House of Representatives in 1973. After three years in the House, she ran for a seat in Maine's Senate, where she focused a great deal of attention on health care issues.

Snowe was first elected to the U.S. Congress in 1978 at the age of thirty-one. While in the House, she was very active with the Congressional Caucus on Women's Issues and served as the caucus co-chair (along with Representative Pat Schroeder) for several years. She was the ranking Republican (the member with the most seniority) on the Subcommittee on Human Services, part of the House Select Committee on Aging. Snowe also sat on the House Foreign Affairs Committee.

Today, Senator Snowe is continuing her work in the area of women's issues, health care, and foreign affairs.

Kay Bailey Hutchison

Kay Bailey Hutchison (R–Tex.; sen. 1993–) is nothing if not a fighter. After winning a special election to the

U.S. Senate, Hutchison made national headlines when she was indicted on charges ranging from abusing her powers as a state official to striking a staff member with a notebook. But Hutchison hails from Texas, a state known for its "anything can happen" politics.

Hutchison was only twenty-nine years old when she was first elected to the Texas State Legislature in 1972. She found she liked politics. Her outside persona of "a very nice girl" hid her tenacity and political savvy. As a state legislator she often joined forces with another legislator, Sarah Weddington (the lawyer in *Roe v. Wade*, the famous case leading to the legalization of abortion). Together they supported bills outlining protective measures for victims of sexual offenses.

In 1990 Hutchison ran for state treasurer and won. Her chance at a national office came soon after, in 1993. Texas Senator Lloyd Bentsen was leaving his seat to join President Clinton's Cabinet. To temporarily fill the spot, Texas Governor Ann Richards appointed Democrat Bob Krueger in June 1993, knowing he would face a special election just a few months later. Hutchison saw her opportunity. She ran a top-notch campaign and beat Krueger by a stunning 67 percent, one of the largest margins in Texas history.

After her election, Senator Hutchison returned to Texas to face the charges leveled against her. She was acquitted of all charges in February 1994. With no time to waste, she had to prepare for another election for a full six-year Senate term. That election, in November 1994, sent her back to Washington with 61 percent of the vote.

Senator Hutchison is considered a loyal Republican Party member, but she votes her conscience on many issues, especially those relating to women. For instance, she supports abortion rights with certain

Newly elected senator Kay Bailey Hutchison meeting with then Senate minority leader Robert Dole in June 1993

limitations, yet she refused to support a bill by Senator Mikulski that would have allowed Medicaid coverage of abortions. She broke rank with party leaders when she refused to vote in favor of allowing Admiral Frank B. Kelso II (who had been involved in the Tailhook scandal) to retire at full rank. In this act of rebellion, Hutchison joined the other women senators, all Democrats.

She sits on four Senate committees, including Armed Services and Commerce, Science and Transportation. In addition, Senator Hutchison is a regional whip for the Republican Party and sits on the National Republican Senatorial Committee.

The Struggle Continues

Women's issues in general have not fared well in the 104th Congress. Abortion is still a very divisive issue, and several bills have been discussed that would limit a woman's right to have an abortion. Workplace and family issues have taken a back seat to pressing financial issues such as the drive to balance the national budget. With the departure of Representative Schroeder and Senator Kassebaum and other congresswomen who have chosen to retire, the future of women's leadership is in question. "There are some matters that have received attention only because of the presence of senior women in positions of power," said Representative Marge Roukema (R–N.J.; rep. 1981–) in a 1995 interview.[1]

But the future on the local level looks bright. More women than ever are being elected to local, county, and state governments. Grassroots organizations are still active, and fundraising groups like EMILY and WISH continue to support women candidates.

True change comes slowly, often taking two steps forward and one step back. Women in Congress have proven they have staying power and the talent to be successful lawmakers. Their effect on American politics has yielded very important change. Where issues of children, working parents, day care, and equal opportunity for women once seemed destined to remain in the shadows, women legislators have brought them into the public eye.

Now we can turn our sights toward a future in which women and men serve the public equally, with each person bringing to public office a unique sense of personal experience and leadership. Then our representatives in Washington will be truly representative of the nation they serve.

How Does Congress Work?

How Congress works may seem like a mystery to some of us. In reality, the rules and activities of Congress are steeped in a tradition envisioned by the framers of the Constitution. This document outlined the United States Congress. It's a credit to the likes of Thomas Jefferson that the Congress described in the Constitution more than two hundred years ago mirrors the Congress of today.

The Two Houses of Congress

Our federal government has three branches: the Executive Branch, or the presidential administration (also referred to as the White House because of the president's residence); the Judiciary Branch, or the Supreme Court; and the Legislative Branch, or Congress.

There are two houses in Congress: the House of Representatives and the Senate. Each maintains its own set of rules, traditions, and reputations. For instance, the Senate is known for having more senior members while the House often has a number of members who have never before served in national politics. Because many representatives move to the Senate after serving in the House for several years, they come with a good working knowledge of the ways of Washington, D.C.

From the very first Congress in 1789, each consecutive Congress has been numbered. In January 1995, the 104th Congress began its session. Each Congress is for two years and generally consists of two sessions, one per year. Elections are held in even years. The first session of a Congress begins at noon on January 3 of the year following the election. For instance, in 1992 elections were held in November, and the 103rd Congress began its first session on January 3, 1993. Elections were held again in November 1994 and the next Congress began on January 3, 1995. In contemporary congresses, each session has short breaks built into it, called recesses, to observe holidays or let members return to their districts and meet with constituents.

Elections and terms for the House and Senate differ. In the House of Representatives everyone serves a two-year term. Therefore, the entire House membership is up for election at the same time. The number of new representatives voted in depends on the mood of the voters; in elections when the country seeks a change, fewer incumbent representatives get reelected. In the Senate, terms are six years. Only one-third of the senators are up for reelection during any one election year. This way, the Senate retains much more continuity. Perhaps this is why the Senate is known for its tradition and its slower pace when considering legislation.

Not everyone can become a member of Congress; representatives and senators must meet certain basic qualifications. For the House, a candidate must be at least twenty-five years old and must have been a United States citizen for seven years. A senatorial candidate must be at least thirty years old and must have been a citizen for nine years. All members must live in the district or state that they represent. No member may hold another federal office while in Congress. Other than these basic requirements, there are few restrictions.

The Two-Party System

Technically, there is no limit to how many political parties may have members in Congress. For most of the country's history, though, two parties have retained most or all of the seats in Congress. Throughout the twentieth century the Republican (sometimes call the Grand Old Party, or GOP) and Democratic parties have been dominant. In order to understand the whats and whys of Congress, it's important to know which party has a majority. It is also important to know to which party the president belongs. Since most legislation is crafted along party lines and ideologies, for a bill to pass, the party must band together and get its members to vote appropriately. If the Democrats are in the White House but not the majority party in the House or Senate, then Democratic legislation will generally have a hard time getting anywhere. This was the case with the 104th Congress: President Bill Clinton was a Democrat who did battle with the Republican leaders of the Senate and the House—Robert Dole and Newt Gingrich, respectively.

Likewise, since the Republicans had a majority in both houses of Congress, they were able to pass a great deal of legislation. The president, though, can always veto it and send it back to Congress.

Congressional votes sometimes fall outside party lines. If individual members of Congress feel strongly about an issue, they may defy party leaders and vote according to their conscience. Controversial issues such as abortion often find members voting on an individual basis rather than according to party ideology. Sometimes pressure from colleagues or lobbying groups can also sway a member's vote.

The leadership of each branch of government can have a great impact on the direction of the country. Yet these leaders are elected to higher posts within their parties by their peers in Congress, not by the voters. Both parties gather their members together on a regular basis to discuss legislation, committee assignments, and other business.

The House of Representatives

There are 435 voting members of the House of Representatives and five non-voting delegates (The District of Columbia, Puerto Rico, Guam, American Samoa, and the Virgin Islands). The House is very different from the Senate and enjoys a history and personality all its own. Although many people consider the Senate a seat of higher power, they would be underestimating the direct influence on American domestic and foreign policy enjoyed by the House.

The House of Representatives has several leadership posts that are filled by the leaders of both political parties. These leaders wield immense power and persuasion both in the chamber and behind office doors.

Speaker of the House is the top job in the House of Representatives. The Speaker is elected by the representatives and is almost always the leader of the majority party. The Speaker's major responsibilities are: to preside over the House and direct parliamentary procedure; to refer bills to committees; to appoint members to special committees or assignments; and to act as the leader and spokesperson of the majority party. The Speaker is also second in the line of succession to the presidency (following the vice president) should the president die or become incapacitated. The Speaker does not usually vote on bills or amendments except to break a tie.

Another important leadership position is **Majority Leader,** who formulates the party's legislative program and is always the first to be recognized on the floor of the chamber. The **Minority Leader** acts as a counter to the majority's agenda and acts as the spokesperson for her or his party.

Then come the **Party Whips.** Whip comes from a British hunting term, "whipper-in," which is used to describe the person responsible for keeping the hounds from leaving the pack on a fox hunt. This is a very apt description, as the role of a party whip is to keep members in line and make sure they will be voting as the party wishes. Whips are appointed by their party's leaders.

The Senate

In the Senate the leadership positions are slightly different, because the workings of this body are different. In the House the number of representatives is based on the population in each state; large states like California and New York may have twenty or thirty representatives, while less populous states like Hawaii or Vermont may have just three or four. In the Senate, each state enjoys equal representation—two senators apiece. A state's senator with the most seniority is referred to as the "senior senator" and the one with less experience the "junior senator." For instance, Nancy Kassebaum of Kansas was elected senator in 1978, but her partner, Robert Dole, was first elected in 1969. As the Senate floor leader, Dole would recognize Senator Kassebaum not with her name but rather with the response, "I now recognize the junior senator from Kansas."

The Vice President of the United States presides over the Senate and is first in the line of succession to the presidency. But the vice president does not vote on bills in the Senate, except in the rare occasion of breaking a tie.

The **president *pro tempore*** (or *pro tem*) of the Senate is third in the line of presidential succession. This person presides over the Senate when the vice president is not available. (The term *pro tempore* means "for the time being"; that is, this person is president of the Senate just while the vice president is away.) She or he also recognizes senators to speak on the floor, decides points of order, and makes appointments to the Senate-House joint committees. The president *pro tempore* can also appoint members to sit on special committees.

The most powerful leader in the Senate is the **Majority Leader**. This is the person who leads the majority party and schedules when votes will come to the floor. The success of a session of Congress is often determined by the skill and vision of the majority leaders in both houses. There are also **Senate Whips** who have similar duties to their counterparts in the House.

Congressional Committees

The House and Senate conduct much of their legislative business in committee. It's here that research is conducted, preliminary votes are taken, and decisions are made about what legislation to consider. Both houses of Congress have standing committees and select or special committees, and each committee has several sub-committees specializing in one or two areas. For instance, Labor Standards, Occupational Health and Safety is the name of just one subcommittee of the Labor and Human Resources Committee of the Senate.

Following is a list of the congressional committees in the 104th Congress. Note that in addition to four joint committees, there are several issues that are covered in committees in both houses.

SENATE COMMITTEES
Aging
Agriculture, Nutrition, and Forestry
Appropriations
Armed Services
Banking, Housing, and Urban Affairs
Budget
Commerce, Science, and Transportation
Energy and Natural Resources
Environment and Public Works
Ethics
Finance
Foreign Relations
Governmental Affairs
Indian Affairs
Intelligence
Judiciary
Labor and Human Resources
Rules and Administration
Small Business
Veterans' Affairs

JOINT COMMITTEES
Economic
Library
Printing
Taxation

HOUSE COMMITTEES
Agriculture
Appropriations
Banking and Financial Services
Budget
Commerce
Economic and Educational Opportunities
Government Reform and Oversight
House Oversight
Intelligence
International Relations
Judiciary
National Security
Resources
Rules
Science
Small Business
Standards of Official Conduct
Transportation and Infrastructure
Veterans' Affairs
Ways and Means

HOW AN IDEA BECOMES A LAW

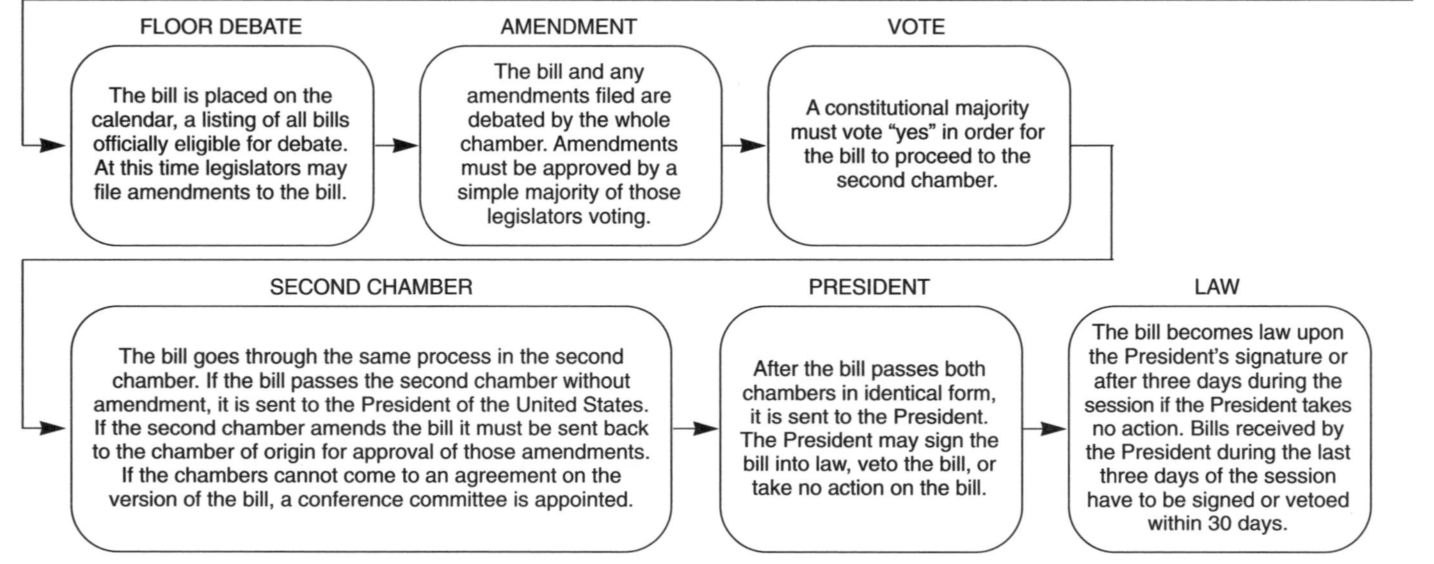

The Legislative Process

The process of creating and passing legislation is cumbersome and, at times, needlessly long. Before an idea can become law it travels quite a distance, stopping on the way as legislators study it, have the public voice their thoughts, determine how much it will cost, and finally vote on it—maybe. The Constitution outlines these safeguards and checkpoints. This is to assure that no one person or party becomes too powerful.

The ideas for laws come from four major sources:

1. **The Administration**—The president can ask staff and assistants to draft legislation, such as an annual budget. But since bills can only be introduced by a member of Congress, any legislation drafted by the president must be introduced by someone else.

2. **Constituents**—Any citizen or group of citizens can approach their representative and ask for assistance in getting a bill introduced and passed. Sometimes this will concern a local issue, such as building an expressway. Sometimes the issue has to do with social programs, like getting money appropriated to fund housing or help the poverty-stricken.

3. **Lobbying Organizations**—In today's political arena there are literally hundreds of different lobbying organizations, each concerned with a well-defined issue or area of concern. They run the gamut of interests and ideologies: the National Rifle Association lobbies congressmembers to ease gun control laws; the National Organization for Women lobbies for women's rights and issues; the National Gay and Lesbian Task Force lobbies for gay and lesbian civil rights; the Heritage Foundation is concerned with conservative Christian issues. There are also groups that lobby on behalf of business concerns. Cigarette makers back the tobacco lobby, insurance companies have banded

together to send lobbyists to Washington, and even Hollywood sends people to voice its concerns.

Lobbying groups will often draft their own legislation and then find a member to introduce it and be its sponsor on the floor. In recent years lobbying groups have come under fire because of the power they use (and sometimes abuse). Lobbying groups often donate money or gifts to members of Congress. In turn, that member may feel beholden to the group's bidding. (Some members like Margaret Chase Smith refused to take any large donations from any groups because she did not want to feel indebted to anyone.)

4. **Members of Congress**—Many representatives and senators come to Washington with ideas for laws or programs that they would like to see enacted. They will draft a bill, introduce it, and work with other members to gain their support. Because compromise and coalition are the stuff of politics, members will often work in association with other representatives and senators— "I'll support your bill if you support mine."

Once a bill is drafted and introduced it is given a number. If it comes from the House of Representatives that number begins with HR, if from the Senate it begins with S. Then the bill is sent to the appropriate committee, where the real work begins.

Committees decide which of the bills sent to them will be considered. Sometimes research is conducted or hearings held to learn more about the issue and to see if the proposed piece of legislation will solve the problem. Committees will also discern the financial impact of the bill. Committees, and especially their chairpersons, enjoy a great deal of power when evaluating proposed legislation. One can see why committee assignments are so important and such a strong gauge of congressional influence. Women have been struggling for decades to get access to this power, to be given good committee assignments and to become committee chairs.

Bills are often "killed in committee," meaning that the committee chair decides not to even consider it or that committee members feel the bill is not satisfactory. They could also make changes to a bill before sending it on to the full chamber (either the House or Senate). Its next step would be a vote by the full body, but here, too, a bill can die. If the Speaker of the House or the Senate Majority Leader decides not to bring it up for a vote, then the bill will die at the end of that congressional session.

Let's say that we have introduced a bill to fund college assistance for low-income students. A version of our bill is introduced in the House. It gets sent to the Education and Labor Committee for review. After about six months of consideration and research, the committee votes to recommend the program. Okay, our bill has made it over one hurdle. Now it's got to find its way to a vote on the House floor.

If the Speaker of the House supports this issue, he puts it on the legislative schedule so it can come up for a vote. Members then debate the merits of the program, give speeches and then vote. Our bill, we'll say, passes by a wide margin. This is not an easy feat, considering the number of bills introduced in each session. During the 101st Congress (1989 to 1991), for instance, almost 12,000 bills were introduced, but only 650 of these made it through the process to become law.

To continue our scenario: A slightly different version of our bill was introduced simultaneously in the Senate. There it went through similar scrutiny and landed in the Labor and Human Resources Committee. It was passed in both committee and Senate floor votes. Now it must go to a joint "conference" committee to be reconciled—the Senate and the House have to combine it into one bill.

If our bill is among the few successful ones, it will get sent to the president. It is at this point that the president either signs the bill into law or vetoes it. If he chooses the latter, our bill will likely go back to Congress for another vote. If it passes by a two-thirds majority the president's veto is overridden and the bill will become law.

Making laws is just one of Congress's tasks. It also approves candidates for the Supreme Court and appointments to the various cabinet committees and departments through the Senate Judiciary Committee. It influences foreign policy, holds public hearings on a variety of issues, and is in charge of investigating the alleged wrongdoing of its own members. Perhaps the most important role of Congress is to lead the country and set it on a path for the future.

The Complete Roster of Women in Congress

REPRESENTATIVE	PARTY	STATE	YEARS IN OFFICE
Jeannette Rankin	R	Montana	1917–19, 1942–43
Alice Mary Robertson	R	Oklahoma	1921–23
Winifred Sprague Mason Huck	R	Illinois	1922–23
Mae Ella Nolan	R	California	1923–25
Florence P. Kahn	R	California	1925–37
Mary T. Norton	D	New Jersey	1925–51
Edith Nourse Rogers	R	Massachusetts	1925–60
Katherine Langley	R	Kentucky	1927–31
Pearl P. Oldfield	D	Arkansas	1929–31
Ruth Hanna McCormick	R	Illinois	1929–31
Ruth Bryan Owen	D	Florida	1929–33
Ruth Baker Pratt	R	New York	1929–33
Effiegene Wingo	D	Arkansas	1930–33
Willa B. Eslick	D	Tennessee	1932–33
Virginia Ellis Jenckes	D	Indiana	1933–39
Kathryn O'Loughlin McCarthy	D	Kansas	1933–35
Marian Williams Clarke	R	New York	1934–35
Isabella Greenway	D	Arizona	1934–37
Caroline O'Day	D	New York	1935–43
Nan Wood Honeyman	D	Oregon	1937–39
Jessie Sumner	R	Illinois	1937–47
Elizabeth H. Gasque	D	South Carolina	1939
Clara G. McMillan	D	South Carolina	1940–41
Florence R. Gibbs	D	Georgia	1940–41
Frances P. Bolton	R	Ohio	1940–69
Margaret Chase Smith*	R	Maine	1940–49
Katharine Edgar Byron	D	Maryland	1941–43

REPRESENTATIVE	PARTY	STATE	YEARS IN OFFICE
Veronica Boland	D	Pennsylvania	1942–43
Clare Boothe Luce	R	Connecticut	1943–47
Winifred C. Stanley	R	New York	1943–45
Willa L. Fulmer	D	South Carolina	1944–45
Emily Taft Douglas	D	Illinois	1945–47
Helen Gahagan Douglas	D	California	1945–51
Chase Going Woodhouse	D	Connecticut	1945–47, 1949–51
Helen Douglas Mankin	D	Georgia	1946–47
Eliza Jane Pratt	D	North Carolina	1946–47
Georgia L. Lusk	D	New Mexico	1947–49
Katharine St. George	R	New York	1947–65
Reva Beck Bosone	D	Utah	1949–53
Cecil M. Harden	R	Indiana	1949–59
Edna F. Kelly	D	New York	1949–69
Vera Buchanan	D	Pennsylvania	1951–55
Maude Elizabeth Kee	D	West Virginia	1951–65
Marguerite Stitt Church	R	Illinois	1951–63
Ruth Thompson	R	Michigan	1951–57
Leonor K. Sullivan	D	Missouri	1953–77
Gracie Pfost	D	Idaho	1953–63
Mary Elizabeth Farrington	R	Hawaii	1954–57
Iris Blitch	D	Georgia	1955–63
Edith Green	D	Oregon	1955–75
Martha Griffiths	D	Michigan	1955–75
Coya Knutson	D	Minnesota	1955–59
Kathryn Granahan	D	Pennsylvania	1956–63
Florence P. Dwyer	R	New Jersey	1957–72
Catherine May	R	Washington	1959–70
Edna Simpson	R	Illinois	1959–61
Jessie McCullough Weis	R	New York	1959–63
Julia Butler Hansen	D	Washington	1960–75
Louise G. Reece	R	Tennessee	1961–63
Catherine D. Norrell	D	Arkansas	1961–63
Corinne Boyd Riley	D	South Carolina	1962–63
Charlotte T. Reid	R	Illinois	1963–71
Irene B. Baker	R	Tennessee	1964–65
Patsy T. Mink	D	Hawaii	1965–77, 1990–
Lera M. Thomas	D	Texas	1966–67
Margaret M. Heckler	R	Massachusetts	1967–82

REPRESENTATIVE	PARTY	STATE	YEARS IN OFFICE
Shirley A. Chisholm	D	New York	1969–80
Bella Abzug	D	New York	1971–76
Ella T. Grasso	D	Connecticut	1971–75
Louise D. Hicks	D	Massachusetts	1971–73
Barbara Jordan	D	Texas	1973–79
Elizabeth Andrews	D	Alabama	1973
Yvonne Brathwaite Burke	D	California	1973–79
Patricia Schroeder	D	Colorado	1973–97
Cardiss Collins	D	Illinois	1973–97
Corinne "Lindy" Boggs	D	Louisiana	1973–91
Marjorie S. Holt	R	Maryland	1973–87
Elizabeth Holtzman	D	New York	1973–81
Shirley N. Pettis	R	California	1975–79
Martha Keys	D	Kansas	1975–79
Gladys Noon Spellman	D	Maryland	1975–79
Virginia Smith	R	Nebraska	1975–91
Millicent Fenwick	R	New Jersey	1975–83
Helen Stevenson Meyner	D	New Jersey	1975–79
Marilyn Lloyd	D	Tennessee	1975–94
Mary Rose Oakar	D	Ohio	1977–93
Barbara Mikulski*	D	Maryland	1977–86
Olympia Snowe*	R	Maine	1979–94
Beverly B. Bryon	D	Maryland	1979–93
Geraldine Ferraro	D	New York	1979–85
Bobbi Fiedler	R	California	1981–87
Marge Roukema	R	New Jersey	1981–
Jean Ashbrook	R	Ohio	1981–83
Lynn Martin	R	Illinois	1981–91
Katie Hall	D	Indiana	1981–85
Claudine Schneider	R	Rhode Island	1981–90
Barbara B. Kennelly	D	Connecticut	1983–
Nancy L. Johnson	R	Connecticut	1983–
Barbara Boxer*	D	California	1983–93
Sala Burton	D	California	1983–89
Barbara F. Vucanovich	R	Nevada	1983–97
Marcy Kaptur	D	Ohio	1983–
Jan Meyers	R	Kansas	1985–97
Catherine S. Long	D	Louisiana	1985–87
Helen Delich Bentley	R	Maryland	1985–94
Patricia F. Saiki	R	Hawaii	1987–90
Constance A. Morella	R	Maryland	1987–

REPRESENTATIVE	PARTY	STATE	YEARS IN OFFICE
Louise M. Slaughter	D	New York	1987–
Elizabeth J. Patterson	D	South Carolina	1987–93
Nancy Pelosi	D	California	1987–
Jill L. Long	D	Indiana	1989–95
Jolene Unsoeld	D	Washington	1989–95
Joan Kelly Horn	D	Missouri	1991–93
Eleanor Holmes Norton	D	Washington, D.C.	1991–95
Karen English	D	Arizona	1993
Blanche Lambert Lincoln	D	Arkansas	1993–97
Lynn Woolsey	D	California	1993–
Anna G. Eshoo	D	California	1993–
Lucille Roybal-Allard	D	California	1993–
Jane Harman	D	California	1993–
Lynn Schenk	D	California	1993
Corrine Brown	D	Florida	1993–
Tillie Fowler	R	Florida	1993–
Karen L. Thurman	D	Florida	1993–
Carrie Meek	D	Florida	1993–
Cynthia McKinney	D	Georgia	1993–
Pat Danner	D	Missouri	1993–
Nydia M. Velazquez	D	New York	1993–
Carolyn B. Maloney	D	New York	1993–
Eva Clayton	D	North Carolina	1993–
Deborah Pryce	R	Ohio	1993–
Marjorie Margolies-Mezumsky	D	Pennsylvania	1993–95
Karen Shepherd	D	Utah	1993–95
Leslie L. Byrne	D	Virginia	1993–95
Jennifer Dunn	R	Washington	1993–
Maria Cantwell	D	Washington	1993–95
Cleo Fields	D	Louisiana	1993–95
Zoe Lofgren	D	California	1995–
Andrea Seastrand	R	California	1995–
Helen Chenoweth	R	Idaho	1995–
Lynn Rivers	D	Michigan	1995–
Karen McCarthy	D	Missouri	1995–
Sue W. Kelly	R	New York	1995–
Sue Myrick	R	North Carolina	1995–
Elizabeth Furse	D	Oregon	1995–
Sheila Jackson Lee	D	Texas	1995–
Enid Green Waldholtz	R	Utah	1995–97

REPRESENTATIVE	PARTY	STATE	YEARS IN OFFICE
Linda Smith	R	Washington	1995–
Barbara Cubin	R	Wyoming	1995–
Barbara-Rose Collins	D	Michigan	1995–
Rosa DeLauro	D	Connecticut	1995–
Eddie Bernice Johnson	D	Texas	1995–
Nancy Johnson	R	Connecticut	1995–
Nita Lowey	D	New York	1995–
Susan Molinari	R	New York	1995–
Ileana Ros-Lehtinen	R	Florida	1995–
Maxine Waters	D	California	1995–

SENATOR	PARTY	STATE	YEARS IN OFFICE
Rebecca L. Felton	Ind. D	Georgia	1922
Hattie W. Caraway	D	Arkansas	1931–45
Rose McConnell Long	D	Louisiana	1936
Dixie Bibb Graves	D	Alabama	1938–39
Gladys Pyle	R	South Dakota	1938–39
Vera Bushfield	R	South Dakota	1948–49
Margaret Chase Smith*	R	Maine	1949–73
Eva Bowring	R	Nebraska	1954
Hazel Abel	R	Nebraska	1954–55
Maurine B. Neuberger	D	Oregon	1961–67
Elaine Edwards	D	Louisiana	1972
Maryon Pittman Allen	D	Alabama	1978
Nancy L. Kassebaum	R	Kansas	1978–97
Muriel Buck Humphrey	D	Minnesota	1978–83
Paula Hawkins	R	Florida	1981–87
Barbara Mikulski*	D	Maryland	1986–
Jocelyn Burdick	D	North Dakota	1991–92
Dianne Feinstein	D	California	1992–
Barbara Boxer*	D	California	1992–
Carol Moseley Braun	D	Illinois	1992–
Patty Murray	D	Washington	1992–
Kay Bailey Hutchison	R	Texas	1993–
Olympia Snowe*	R	Maine	1994–

*Has served in both houses of Congress.

(Some statistics courtesy of the Center for the American Woman and Politics, Eagleton Institute of Politics, Rutgers University)

Source Notes

Chapter 1—Jeannette Rankin: The First Woman in Congress

1. Chamberlain, Hope, *A Minority of Members* (New York: Praeger Publishers, 1973), p. 8.

2. Chamberlain, p. 7.

3. Chamberlain, p. 18.

Chapter 2—The Early Years

1. Chamberlain, Hope, *A Minority of Members* (New York: Praeger Publishers, 1973), p. 79.

2. Chamberlain, p. 36.

3. Chamberlain, p. 45.

4. Chamberlain, p. 39.

Chapter 3—Family Connections

1. Witt, Linda, et al, *Running as a Woman* (New York: Free Press, 1993), p. 96.

Chapter 4—Margaret Chase Smith

1. Gertzog, Irwin, *Congressional Women* (New York: Praeger Publishers, 1984), p. 159.

2. Lamson, Peggy, *Few are Chosen* (Boston: Houghton Mifflin, 1968), p. 12.

3. Graham, Frank, Jr. *Margaret Chase Smith: Woman of Courage* (New York: John Day Co., 1964), p. 176.

4. Wallace, Patricia Ward, *Margaret Chase Smith: Politics of Conscience* (Westport, Conn.: Praeger Publishers, 1995), p. 109.

5. Wallace, p. 160.

6. "Margaret Chase Smith is Dead at 97; Maine Republican Made History Twice." *New York Times,* May 30, 1995.

Chapter 5—Decades of Change

1. Witt, Linda, et al, *Running as a Woman* (New York: Free Press, 1993), p.229.

2. Lamson, Peggy, *Few are Chosen* (Boston: Houghton Mifflin, 1968), p. 108.

3. LeVeness, Frank P., and Jane P. Sweeney, eds., *Women Leaders in Contemporary U.S. Politics* (Boulder, Colo.: Lynne Reinner Publishers, 1987), p. 13.

4. Gilbert, Lynn, and Gaylen Moore, *Particular Passions* (New York: Clarkson N. Potter Publishers, 1981), p. 186.

5. Gilbert and Moore, p. 188.

6. Abzug, Bella, *Gender Gap* (Boston: Houghton Mifflin, 1984), p. 161.

7. Abzug, Bella, *Bella! Ms. Abzug Goes to Washington* (New York: Saturday Review Press, 1972), p.3.

8. Butler, Phyllis, and Dorothy Gray. *Everywoman's Guide to Political Awareness* (Millbrae, Calif.: Les Femmes, 1976), p. 70.

9. Clines, Francis X., "Barbara Jordan, a Lawmaker of Resonant Voice, Dies at 59." *New York Times,* January 18, 1996.

10. Ivins, Molly, *Molly Ivins Can't Say That Can She?* (New York: Random House, 1991), p. 1.

11. Foehr, Stephen, "Not Standing Pat: Leaving Congress, Schroeder seeks a new way to awaken womankind," *Chicago Tribune,* February 11, 1996, p. 3.

Chapter 6—Getting Together: The Congressional Caucus on Women's Issues

1. Dunham, Richard, "Ms. Smith Goes to Washington; Women lawmakers are changing the shape of Congress." *Business Week,* September 26, 1994, p. 96.

Chapter 7—Geraldine Ferraro

1. LeVeness, Frank P., and Jane P. Sweeney, eds., *Women Leaders in Contemporary U.S. Politics* (Boulder, Colo., Lynne Rienner Publishers, 1987), p. 41.

2. Ferraro, Geraldine A., with Linda Bird Francke, *Ferraro, My Story* (New York: Bantam Books, 1985), p. 262.

3. Hicks, Jonathan P., "After Retreating From Politics, Ferraro is Talking About Another Try," *New York Times,* January 16, 1996, p. A13.

Chapter 8—Women in the Senate

1. Chamberlain, Hope, *A Minority of Members* (New York: Praeger Publishers, 1973), p. 199.

2. Boxer, Barbara, *Strangers in the Senate* (Washington, D.C.: National Press Book, 1994), p. 119.

3. Witt, Linda, et al., *Running as a Woman* (New York: Free Press, 1993), p. 271.

Chapter 9—1992: The Year of the Woman

1. *Primetime Live*, July 1992.

2. *Primetime Live*, July 1992.

3. *Time*, August 16, 1993, p. 12.

Chapter 10—Congress Today

1. Phinney, David, "Exodus of women shakes up Congress." *San Francisco Examiner*, November 30, 1995.

For More Information

FOR FURTHER READING

Abzug, Bella. *Gender Gap*. Boston: Houghton Mifflin, 1984.

Abzug, Bella. *Bella! Ms. Abzug Goes to Washington*. New York: Saturday Review Press, 1972.

Boxer, Barbara. *Strangers in the Senate: Politics and the New Revolution of Women in America*. Washington, D.C.: National Press Book, 1994.

Burrell, Barbara. *A Woman's Place Is in the House*. Ann Arbor, Mich.: University of Michigan Press, 1994.

Bryant, Ira. *Barbara Charline Jordan: From the Ghetto to the Capitol*. Houston: D. Armstrong Co., 1977.

Carroll, Susan. *Women as Candidates in American Politics*. Bloomington, Ind.: Indiana University Press, 1994.

Chamberlin, Hope. *A Minority of Members*. New York: Praeger Publishers, 1973.

Clines, Francis X. "Barbara Jordan, a Lawmaker of Resonant Voice, Dies at 59." *New York Times*, January 18, 1996.

Congressional Quarterly, Inc. Staff. *How Congress Works*. Washington, D.C.: Congressional Quarterly, 1991.

Englebarts, Rudolf. *Women in the United States Congress 1917–1972*. Littleton, Colo.: Libraries Unlimited, Inc., 1974.

Ferraro, Geraldine. *Changing History: Women, Power, and Politics*. Wakefield, R.I.: Moyer Bell, 1993.

Ferraro, Geraldine A., with Linda Bird Francke. *Ferraro, My Story*. New York: Bantam Books, 1985.

Foehr, Stephen. "Not Standing Pat: Leaving Congress, Schroeder seeks a new way to awaken womankind." *Chicago Tribune*, February 11, 1996.

Gertzog, Irwin. *Congressional Women: Their Recruitment, Treatment and Behavior*. New York: Praeger Publishers, 1995.

Gilbert, Lynn, and Gaylen Moore. *Particular Passions*. New York: Clarkson N. Potter Publishers, 1981.

Gruberg, Martin. *Women in American Politics*. Oshkosh, Wis.: Academia Press, 1968.

Hartmann, Susan M. *From Margin to Mainstream: American Women in Politics since 1960*. New York: Alfred A. Knopf, 1989.

Haskins, James. *Barbara Jordan*. New York: Dial Press, 1977.

Hicks, Jonathan P. "After Retreating From Politics, Ferraro is Talking About Another Try." *New York Times*, January 16, 1996.

Ivins, Molly. *Molly Ivins Can't Say That, Can She?* New York: Random House, 1991.

Jordan, Barbara, and Shelby Hearon. *A Self-Portrait*. Garden City, N.Y.: Doubleday & Co., 1979.

Kunin, Madeleine M. *Living a Political Life*. New York: Alfred A. Knopf, 1994.

Lamson, Peggy. *Few Are Chosen: American Women in Political Life Today*. Boston: Houghton Mifflin, 1968.

Lawson, Don. *Geraldine Ferraro: The Woman who Changed American Politics*. New York: Julian Messner, 1985.

LeVeness, Frank P., and Jane P. Sweeney, eds. *Women Leaders in Contemporary U.S. Politics*. Boulder, Colo.: Lynne Rienner Publishers, 1987.

Mandel, Ruth. *In the Running: The New Woman Candidate*. Boston: Beacon Press, 1983.

McCullough, Joan. *First of All: Significant "Firsts" by American Women*. New York: Holt Rinehart & Winston, 1980.

Phinney, David. "Exodus of women shakes up Congress." *San Francisco Examiner*, November 30, 1995.

Schroeder, Patricia S., and Andrea Camp. *Champion of the Great American Family: A Personal and Political Book*. New York: Random House, 1989.

Wallace, Patricia Ward. *Margaret Chase Smith: Politics of Conscience*. Westport, Conn: Praeger Publishers, 1995.

Whitney, Sharon, and Tom Raynor. *Women in Politics*. New York: Franklin Watts, 1986.

Witt, Linda, et al. *Running as a Woman: Gender and Power in American Politics*. New York: Free Press, 1993.

POLITICAL ADDRESSES ON THE WORLD WIDE WEB

Due to the changeable nature of the Internet, sites appear and disappear very quickly. Following are examples of the myriad of resources that provide useful information on politics, politicians, government, and history. Internet addresses must be entered with capital and lowercase letters exactly as they appear.

http://policy.net
A guide to the U.S. Congress on the World Wide Web

http://thomas.loc.gov
Legislative information organized by the Library of Congress

http://www.whitehouse.gov
The White House

http://www.politicsusa.com
A service of the National Journal and the American Political Network

http://www.lwv.org/~lwvsus
League of Women Voters of the United States

http://www.vote-smart.org
Information on the U.S. House of Representatives and Senate

http://www.senate.gov
United States Senate

http://www.house.gov
United States House of Representatives

http://www.rci.rutgers.edu/~cawp
Center for the American Woman and Politics

To look up a specific topic or conduct a general search, try one of the following search engines:

http://www.yahoo.com
http://www.altavista.digital.com

Index

Page numbers in *italics* refer to illustrations

About the Author

JILL S. POLLACK IS a writer and editor whose work has appeared in newspapers, magazines, trade periodicals, and political journals. A graduate of The George Washington University, Ms. Pollack has worked on political campaigns and with political action committees. She is also the author of *Shirley Chisholm* and *Lesbian & Gay Families: Redefining Parenting in America*, both published by Franklin Watts. She lives in Chicago.